A PREMATURE EULOGY

JOHN BYE

"I was rather hoping to be here today."

I've suffered for my art ... now it's your turn!

(with apologies to the seventh Python , Neil Innes)

A PREMATURE EULOGY

© John Bye, 2021. All rights reserved.

ISBN 978-0-6452898-0-0

Special thanks to Wendy Sutherland,
Jacki Burgess and Richard Opat

Cover artwork: Jamie Coghill. Layout design: Stu Banko

IngramSpark

PREFACE

Here's my motivation for writing this book.

Em, Kysa and Kit

I would say that there is a fair chance that one day
we all may shuffle off this mortal coil.

To make things easier for family and loved ones, I would suggest
that we all think about our final set; spell it out while we still can.
It's not a morbid task, just good planning.

My three daughters are scattered all around Australia.

In 2017 we decided to have an extra long weekend together in Tasmania. We rented a big house overlooking Constitution Dock in Hobart and after settling in, I called a meeting. The silence shrieked, "What's this about?"

I asked the girls to hear me out for a five minute summary of my exit plans,
should that time ever come. After all, at the time I was in my
extremely late fifties. (My next birthday was my seventieth.) I told them
that I had written my own eulogy to save them any discomfort
and that I'm quite happy to make jokes about myself.

It was a little challenging for us all, but totally necessary.
That done, we cracked a bottle of bubbles and the party commenced.

Our conversation moved on to talking about my life before kids
and the girls suggested I write about my early home life and the things
I got up to in my younger days. This project has made a life of its own.

The actual very brief eulogy is not included.

CONTENTS

1	Part the One	1
2	Somers (1951)	6
3	Echuca	10
4	Sundays	14
5	Echuca Primary School	17
6	Summer Holidays	25
7	Sandringham	27
8	The Pre Band Years	30
9	Forming My First band	33
10	Beale Street Jazz Club	37
11	Bay City Jazz Band	42
12	Downbeat Concerts	47
13	High School Blues	50
14	More Gigs	52
15	Ubangi Jazz Band	58
16	Auburn	61
17	Heading West	64
18	Back Home	76
19	Kinderplay	79
20	John Bye Productions	93
21	Guess What?	101
22	Go West Young Family	107
23	Showbits	111
24	Newmarket Music	119
25	Way Beyond Melbourne	127
26	Thee Lady at the Market	130
27	It's Definitely Laos	136
28	Hawaii	140
29	Myanmar	142
30	Who's Scooter?	144
31	Champasak, Laos	146
32	Update Digital	148
33	Monday One Day, Monday the Next	151

1 - PART THE ONE

I'm sure our life is largely mapped out before we arrive on this planet. The setting is not of our own choosing. Reg and Kath prearranged my opening set.

I was born on January 4th 1948, although I don't seem to remember much about that event as I was very young at the time, although my parents were not. My mother was 42 and my father was 45.

At the time King George VI was on the throne (so to speak) and the population of Australia was 7,708,761* (*that's me on the end).

Early in life, I chose to jump in at the deep end and never let a lack of talent get in the way of anything I had in mind. As a teenage kid I always wanted to play the trumpet really badly. I achieved that goal. (Pun intended). I've certainly had my share of disasters, together with a good deal of learning on the job.

Who hasn't?

I feel that if you haven't made a substantial portfolio of mistakes in life, you probably haven't tried hard enough. Sure, we're all different, but I never wanted to sit on the fence or be a passenger. Some junior sports coaches tell their little charges, "We don't lose, we learn". The fact is that sometimes in life, we do lose.

My parents decided my first setting was to be South Yarra, Melbourne, in the first half of last century. On my arrival, they gave me four siblings to get started; all girls. Shirley (2/10/1940), Margaret (25/01/1942), Heather (18/06/1943) and Rosemary (02/11/1944).

In later life I reminded my sisters that our parents kept having kids until they got one they liked.

My mother told me that the first, and thankfully not the last, stupid thing I did was to crawl across Punt Road, South Yarra. Fortunately the traffic stopped and gave way to me with Mum in full flight just behind.

So far, I'd made it to my first birthday. Punt Road was unmade, whereas today it's a major carriageway.

My Parents:
Reginald Frank Pearn Bye 2/7/1902 - 16/10/1972
Kathleen Alma Scholes 14/2/1905 - 19/4/1979

Dad was a Methodist minister and Mum a triple certificated nurse. They met when Mum was nursing Dad's first wife who died very early into their marriage. In later years I joked that Mum had probably topped her. That little attempt at humour didn't go down well.

Mum was the daughter of a Methodist minister, Reverend Samuel Scholes, who later became the chairman of Methodist Ladies College (MLC) in Hawthorn. Mum had two sisters, Lillian and Florence, and a brother, John (aka Jack), who was killed in WW2. Mum's maiden sisters lived together in the big weatherboard family home in Mont Albert, an eastern suburb of Melbourne in the 'dry belt', also referred to as 'the Bible belt'. That suited them. They were totally committed, old school Christians and detested "strong drink". Auntie Lil lectured in Latin and French at Melbourne University. She became the first woman to become an ordained minister of religion in the Anglican Church of Australia.

Mum's younger sister Florence was affectionately called 'Auntie Noy' by us kids, although Mum called her 'Floss'. Florence Scholes came to work in Melbourne University's Law School for three weeks and stayed 38 years. She became personal secretary to Zelman Cowen, dean of the law faculty. He later became Sir Zelman Cowen, and Governor General of Australia.

I always thought of these two aunties as fuddy-duddies. They seemed so much older than our parents. Noy was a soft, gentle soul who ran their household, while Lil was the academic who had no grasp of day-to-day tasks. I seem to remember she was always reading, or writing...and she had whiskers. Mum would say 'give your Auntie Lil a kiss'. OH! No. I didn't like that one little bit. Auntie Noy's purple nose was due to poor circulation, so mum said.

I never got to know any of my grandparents so I guess the two maiden aunts were taking that role, even though they had no maternal instincts, as I recall. I can't ever remember staying over with them, or even wanting to.

My father was born in Barrington, Tasmania. He was the son of a farmer who was a fire and brimstone Baptist 'lay' preacher. Dad had two brothers, Frank and Arthur. Arthur died in WW1 and Frank was
tragically killed at a very young age. It sounds a bit weird, but another brother came along in later life, and he too, was named Frank. Frank (the second) established a very successful confectionery distribution business in Tasmania.

F. R. Bye Pty Ltd had the distribution contracts with major confectionery manufacturers McRobertsons (Cherry Ripe fame) and Hoadleys (Polly Waffle and Violet Crumble fame).

Dad also had two sisters, Ethel and Elsie. Auntie Elsie married late in life. She was a nurse and became romantically attached to a mariner, Gordon Anderson, who was her patient. He had survived a shipboard fall, which left him a paraplegic. They married in 1933 and lived in Rosebud, on the Mornington Peninsula.

Their house was named NODROG, which is Gordon, backwards. He died in 1944. (Incidentally, ROBERTSON PARK backwards is KRAP NOSTREBOR.)

Auntie Elsie moved to the house next door at 5 Wilson Street. My sister, Shirl, and brother-in-law, Geoff, bought that property after her death in the late eighties and lived there for about 25 years.

Our extended family had many happy luncheon parties there and when Lynn and I hooked up in 2003 I took her along to meet the family for the first time. Lynn was so nervous that she had our mutual friend, Monica, come along for support. It was a hoot! Everyone took to Lynn and she was part of our family in no time. I must also document that Lynn's family took me in with similar affection.

Auntie Elsie was a real 'lady', if a little prickly at times. When we went down to Rosebud to visit her, it was like going to High Tea in a fancy Collins Street hotel. We had to wear our Sunday best and Auntie would constantly correct our grammar and generally make everyone feel under scrutiny.

There was an often-told occasion when my sisters took Auntie Elsie for a picnic at Arthur's Seat. They setup the outdoor table with a tablecloth and fancy paper serviettes. A sudden puff of wind took off with the serviettes and sent them airborne. A schoolboy passing by on the way to his bus, picked up and returned the wayward paperwork. Auntie Elsie called out, in her best posh voice, "Good boy, well done". The whole busload of schoolboys echoed, "Good boy, well done", as the bus departed.

Dad's other sister, Ethel, was a very talented artist and in her twilight years played the foot-pumped organ very badly. It screeched and wheezed like an asthmatic squeezebox accordion. Auntie Ethel's fridge had its own eco system. It was not a safe food storage unit.

Dad's grandfather, William Bye, was born in the tiny village of Stow Bedon, Norfolk, U.K. His wife was a 'Prewer' from Breckles, a little village close by. Dad had to work on the farm after school and also had a part time job in a general store. Sunday was 'go to meeting' day.

Dad left the farm in Tasmania as soon as he could and went back to school to get his matriculation and go on to study divinity at Queens College,

University of Melbourne. He became a pillar of the Methodist church in Melbourne. After being involved with the North Melbourne Methodist Mission in the 1940s, he went on to establish the Prahran Methodist Mission in 1946. He arranged the purchase of a property in the heart of Prahran's busy shopping precinct and the local church-shy families were welcomed. The mission offered much more than soup, soap and salvation, and the good work continues to this day. Dad was described as "a man of vision, with a stout heart and the courage of a lion" (The Spectator, 1948).

His extensive workload took a huge toll on his health and he was ordered to take a complete break. The family had access to a little holiday cottage in Somers and in 1951 the seven Byes moved from inner city Melbourne to a tiny cottage in a sleepy beachside hollow on Westernport Bay.

Today, The Prahran Methodist Mission has morphed into Uniting Prahran. www.unitingprahan.org.au

Their mission statement (pun intended) is 'everyone has the right to a decent life'.

I also believe that everyone has the right to a decent end of life.

This is my family in waiting

2 - SOMERS (1951)

Our little cottage was named 'Little Wildings'. It's still there in Tasman Road, but is now behind a tall fence. Our parents ran one of the three general stores in the town. They had no experience in this business, but they had to make a living.

Palm Beach Store was on the curve of Tasman Road, near the yacht club. Potts general store (long gone) was down near the Lord Somers camp and Stones store was up the other end of Tasman Road. It's the only remaining general store in Somers today.

I remember the sign on the garage roof next to our store. It had a policeman with his hand up saying, 'STOP at Palm Beach Store'.

The Bye kids accounted for 18% of the primary school population. It was a one-classroom school and I was the only kid in prep. I could come and go as I liked, in that first year.

Margie tells me that when she was made class monitor while our teacher had to step out. She held up a picture of 'Fluffy the cat', and asked the four youngest kids what was in the picture. Apparently I looked out the window, turned back and said, "Two pine trees". Silly questions...

Auntie Lil's Day Out

Auntie Lil came down to Somers for a very special day out. Mum packed a picnic lunch and we set up camp in the sand dunes just up from the shoreline. Auntie Lil had a nice sheltered spot to read her book. She wasn't one to walk on the sand, let alone go anywhere near the water. She, like Auntie Noy, liked to have her handbag close by at all times.

The girls decided it would be fun to run down the sand dunes and jump directly over the unsuspecting Aunt. Shirl went first, then Margie, and then Heath. All clear. Along came Roie, thundering down the dunes but she stumbled at the last hurdle and landed on top of the startled Aunt. Sand went everywhere; the book and bag went flying. Auntie Lil threw her hands in the air saying, "Go away, you horrid little infants".

The girls were totally thrilled with their performance. Mum said she wasn't, but she loved hearing the story retold, over and over again.

The Bye kids were free-range kids.

We moved from 'Little Wildings' cottage to a relocated house adjacent to the Palm Beach Store. This house was delivered in two sections and joined up on site. It had already lived a full life as a very basic farmhouse and my earliest memory of that house was my mother sitting on the front step in tears. It must have been an overwhelming upheaval in her already massive workload. She managed to rise above the situation and take control without displaying any other traumatic symptoms. She was resilience personified.

On the plus side, we had more rooms and a bigger back yard.

The girls loved climbing the very large banksia tree that commanded prime position in our new back yard. Shirley set up a system of ropes and pulleys to enable an old hammock to be used as a climbing aid, a little like a rope lift as I remember. Shirl and Marg would go as high up the tree as possible. It scared the living daylights out of me just watching them balancing on the upper branches, way above the ground.

Heather was allowed to go to a lesser height, and Roie was only to visit a much lower branch on the huge tree.

Shirley explained to me that I was far too little for this activity. I was officially confined to terra firma. That seemed to be the case all too often being the youngest sibling. To this very day, this is still the case. Yes girls, I AM the youngest sibling.

The short walk to the beach was challenging in bare feet. It wasn't just the burning hot sand, but the bull ants presented a huge threat. These angry red creatures bit hard and held on. Mum would treat just about any bite or scratch with a Reckitt's blue bag. The little cotton mesh bag soon took away the sting and the blue remaining on the wound was proof of injury long after the pain subsided.

The Merricks Creek ran into Westernport Bay just across the road from our house. I was allowed to fish in the creek with a line attached to a bamboo pole and a safety pin as a hook. Mum would bait up the 'hook' and off I'd go. No need to re-bait and no fish to clean.

Dad loved fishing in the bay. He would go floundering and gar fishing with our neighbour and local builder, Ron Fitzgerald, well after dark. They had a car battery on a floating car tyre tube deck to power their underwater pole lights. They would often come home with a bag of fish. They wore rubber wading pants and I thought they were so brave to go into the dark, waist-deep water at night. Who knows what creatures were lurking around looking for a feed?

My sisters were very adventurous and sometimes stepped into dangerous territory. I was too young to join in, the day they burrowed under the wooden flooring of the general store and made a cubby. But to add to the adventure, they lit candles in the confined, poorly ventilated space. I only know that they (and the shop) were lucky to survive to tell their story...again and again.

Somers Circa 1952   *Left to right: Heath, Shirl, Margie and Roie*

The hero of our story

Free range kids

Little Wildings

Auntie Lil's Day

3 - ECHUCA

In 1954 Dad's health was back on track and he went back to his chosen career (his 'calling' as he would say) as a Methodist minister. He was assigned to the Echuca congregation. We moved to #2 Percy Street, Echuca. The parsonage (minister's house) was directly opposite the Methodist church at the entrance to the Murray River Bridge. Next to our house was a rundown church hall. I'm surprised that the girls didn't try to burn that one down. We had an old garden shed in the backyard, a chook pen and a dilapidated car garage. Our house featured two bedrooms, one bathroom, one toilet and a converted sleep-out on the back verandah. The hot water system and the kitchen stove were wood fuelled. There were two open fireplaces, but the one in the posh room was rarely used. A real estate agent would describe it as a 'renovators delightful opportunity'.

The second bedroom slept my three eldest sisters and Roie and I shared the sleep-out. On a windy winter's night the sleep-out was cold and the louvre windows would rattle. Roie would often say out aloud, "My Father is a policeman". "That should scare off any naughty men", she'd tell me.

Bath time was allocated in age order. I was last in and by then the water was only just warm. We often ran out of hot water and mum would boil the kettle and top up the bath. At least we had an indoor toilet, which we didn't in Somers.

Margaret would often die. Well, she'd pretend to die and I'd believe her. She would throw herself onto her bed, writhe around with great dramatic skill, and stop dead still. I would try to revive her while yelling out to mum for help. Margie would open one eye and say she needed a cuddle to be revived. This happened over and over again and it worked every time. I was only about six, after all.

Special occasions, like birthdays, were a real treat. I don't remember many parties as such, but mum would make a sponge cake, we'd have 'MON' lemonade and a Peter's Family Brick ice cream. A choice of two flavours, vanilla or neapolitan, packaged in a waxed cardboard box.

Six O'clock Swill

The population of Echuca was around 5000 in the mid-50s. The bridge in front of our house connected our town to the NSW town of Moama. Victoria had six o'clock closing and NSW allowed hotels to serve alcohol until 10 pm. The bridge was very busy around these times. We were told of the dangers of the demon drink.

One memorable evening my father took me down to the Royal Hotel to witness the six o'clock swill and smell the stale beer emanating from this notorious drinking hole.

At 11 years of age I was encouraged to sign the temperance pledge to abstain from all intoxicating liquors and beverages.

'Lips that touch alcohol shall never touch mine.'

I must have had my fingers crossed on both hands, plus a few toes.

Her Majesty's Visit

Soon after we set up residence, Queen Elizabeth II came to visit Echuca, by train. I was quite impressed with her effort to make us feel welcome. (We knew of her, but we didn't know her, as such.) The railway line right across the road from our house had been upgraded and a special platform built just near the wharf. I went down with the other grade one and two kids and waved my little Aussie flag as hard as I could. I'm not sure if Her Majesty noticed me, but she did smile. She wore white gloves.

The town brass band gave a fine performance as the Royal train headed off. I loved the big bold sound of brass bands. Still do. A year later the mighty Murray and the nearby Campaspe and Goulburn rivers flooded. It was that built up train line that stopped our house from being inundated. "Thank you Marm."

As the floodwaters receded the pools left behind trapped all sorts of fish, mainly European carp. I found an old metal bucket with the bottom rusted through perfect for catching the hapless trapped pests. I took about four decent sized carp home for Mum to cook. She agreed to cook one, if I ate it. That was that. No more of these mud-feeding vermin ever came home.

I loved Saturdays.

We were pretty well given a free run. We did as we pleased...swimming in the river, fishing, footy, climbing things or whatever took our fancy. The girls had no fear. They would swim out to the redgum logs that were being floated down the Murray River to the sawmills. It was so dangerous, but somehow they all survived.

Adjacent to the Evans Bros Redgum sawmill, the rickety old wharf towered above the river. It had been used to service the steamers and barges that plied the Murray River for many, many decades. The girls loved to jump off the top deck and drop the four meters into the muddy water. I only managed to jump from the lower deck. Along the riverbank between the wharf and the pontoon swimming deck there were numerous old, derelict, partly submerged paddle steamers. Many have since been restored and have become Echuca's star tourist attraction.

The Evans sawmill burnt down in February 1959 (nothing to do with my sisters). The whole town turned out that night to experience the spectacular fireworks, but the result was catastrophic for the local economy.

I usually swam in the river near the pontoon pool. I acquired my Herald and Senior swimming certificates there and I once pulled a drowning kid out of the river in that very area. He didn't even thank me. All he did was vomit up gallons of muddy water. It was gross.

I loved to play around the redgum log stockpiles at the Echuca East sawmill with my school mate whose surname was Armstrong. Naturally, I called him Leg-weak. We would squeeze in between the logs and find little hollow areas where we could make a cubby. It really was a stupid, dangerous, exciting way to spend a few hours. Leg-weak had a twin sister who I rather fancied. I'd never had a girlfriend and she kept it that way.

Another favoured pastime was to visit the local tip and see what wonderful things had been thrown out. It was so amazing in the hard rubbish section, not smelly at all, just stuff people didn't value. I found a steering wheel that I modified to fit on my bike. It looked really cool, but it wasn't that easy to steer and balance as I recall. No one else had a bike like mine so it was worth persevering with the added difficulty.

Some Saturday afternoons I was allowed to go to the Paramount Theatre matinee with my mates. There they screened a serial before the feature film. I loved Batman and Robin even though our heroes found themselves in very scary situations and I had to watch through my hand-shielded eyes. During the main feature we rolled Jaffas down the wooden aisles when things slowed down. At the end of the main film they would play the national anthem 'God Save the Queen' with a film showing the new young Queen Elizabeth II sitting on a horse. Everyone would stand up. Most events would include standing for the national anthem. I'm standing now, just thinking about it. Saturday bedtime always came too soon.

The Riverine Herald, 25 November 1959

SCHOOLBOY IN RIVER RESCUE

An Echuca schoolboy who obtained his Education Department senior swimming certificate this year used his knowledge of rescue work to good effect on Monday when he gave assistance to another swimmer who had got into difficulties in the Murray River at Echuca.

The boy is 11-year-old John Bye, the son of Rev. Reg Bye and a pupil at Echuca Central State School.

The boy he rescued, also an 11-year-old, got into difficulties in deep water about 30ft. from the river bank but John was able to assist him to the bank and is to be commended for his courage.

The Temperance Pledge

Echuca Methodist Church and Manse

4 - SUNDAYS

Sundays in the family of a Methodist minister were full on. While many of my mates were out playing by the river or in the parks, my day was mapped out.

In the 1950s there seemed to be rivalry between Protestants and Roman Catholics. I had no idea how to tell the two apart except that the RC nuns and priests all seemed to wear thin wire framed glasses, and looked stern. Maybe there were other differences but that concerned me not.

Here's how my day was to be, each and every Sunday.

9:30am: Christian Endeavour
11:00am: Church
12:30pm: Lunch
2:30pm: Sunday School
7:00pm: Church

We were not permitted to visit the shops. Even if we ran out of bread or milk: too bad. Sunday was a sacred day. I had to keep my Sunday best clothes on, including my tie, until after lunch, and then back on for evening church.

Christian Endeavour

I did not like Christian Endeavour one little bit. It involved learning passages from the Bible and Catechism parrot fashion, without any real understanding of the content.

'I believe in God, the father almighty, creator of heaven and earth...' and so on. (Actually, I don't think I do.)

My CE teacher was not a nice fellow. He was cruel and would often twist my ear if I mucked about. At the end of the tortuous one-hour session my father would come in and recite the benediction. (Closing prayer of which there are 28 with numerous variations) 'May the Lord bless you and keep you...'

Dad always seemed to turn up at the end of any church event and pronounce the benediction. The kids gave me such a hard time over this. "Look, there's your Dad, again!" Dad wore a clerical collar most days and a gown on Sundays. Some kids would ask me why he had his shirt back to front.

'Get used to it, kid. You're going hear this for the next ten years', and I did.

11:00 am Church

Typically, this was a one-hour service. If Dad was conducting a service out in the country, we would have a visiting preacher. Some of these fellows would waffle on and on. It was tedious beyond belief at times.

12:30 pm Lunch

Quite often a local farmer would rock up before church on a Sunday with produce for the minister's family. Fruit, vegetables, sometimes a dead chook complete with feathers. A joint of meat or some industrial strength chops were most welcome at the parsonage. Sunday lunch was a serious event. We were expected to stay in our Sunday church best clothes for what was by today's standards a very formal lunch.

Dad would start with a little religious discussion followed by us all saying grace together.

'For all thy mercies we thank thee, for Christ's sake, Amen'.

My older sisters penned an antidote to the above pre-meal grace.

'Grab all you can and don't think of others'.

Often when Dad gave us a little address before lunch or dinner, a restricted chuckle would come from one of the girls; usually Margaret. Dad would ask, "Who was that?" The others would hold back that real impulse to laugh adding to the blurting noises. Dad would appear to be about to explode, but his eyes gave it away. He was so disciplined. Mum busied herself. Dad had false teeth that clicked as he ate. I had a problem with that, especially when he ate a fresh, crisp apple. That noise still haunts me.

Our parents had a policy of never turning anyone away. It was the 1950s and plenty of people were doing it hard. We had a stream of swaggies who camped under the bridge drop in and ask for something to eat.

That often happened on a Sunday and mum would always rustle up a meal. Quite often this required her to go around the table and collect a little portion from each of our plates. That's just how it was. No one blinked. We had a little table on the back verandah that was always available.

After lunch and the tidy up we could have some free time before heading off to the old hall for 2:30 pm Sunday school.

Our lounge room was our posh room. It always had to be kept tidy and ready for our parents to meet with guests and discuss church business. We had an upright piano in the room and the girls loved to all cram onto the piano bench and play fourhanded chopsticks. Margaret taught me a couple of multi-handed little ditties. I just loved those piano sessions and the laughter that filled our home.

Mum would sometimes play hymns for the women's guild meetings. She preferred to find someone else to play, but she could fumble through the music of the Wesley Brothers. (Not to be confused with the Everly Brothers). Dad would say, "you're a wonder, Kath".

Never in my life did I hear them exchange a harsh word. Each could do no wrong by the other. They had a relationship like no other couple I have ever encountered.

Sunday school was a bit more relaxed than CE but still had set structure. We had typical Bible stories, sang a few churchy songs and the collection plate was passed around while we sang.

'Hear the pennies dropping, listen while they fall, everyone for Jesus, he shall have them all'.

I don't ever remember seeing Jesus collect his pennies. The girls told me that in Somers the school kids sang, 'Jesus loves me, this I know, for the Bye kids tell me so'.

At Sunday school we were divided by age into little groups, for the story-telling sessions. The old hall was noisy with only partitions as walls between all the groups. I didn't mind this, as it was less formal than church or CE.

From about 3:30 pm until 6:00 pm I could change out of my best clobber, and regain my freedom, to a degree. I wasn't allowed to go out kicking a football or being 'boisterous'; after all, it was still Sunday.

After a fairly early dinner, it was back to Church for the 7 pm service. I couldn't wait for the last benediction of the day.

5 - ECHUCA PRIMARY SCHOOL

I quite enjoyed primary school. At playtime the boys would play kick-to-kick football. I remember the older kids were very rough and I often got sent flying while trying to get the ball. The Aboriginal kids were particularly good and one kid in my class went on to play 'A' grade footy in the big league. We also played marbles, but I wasn't much good at that, either. I couldn't get my fingers around the 'cat's eye' and send it hurtling off with any accuracy whatsoever. It usually shot out sideways, costing me the game and my marbles. That's when I first started to lose my marbles.

I liked being the milk monitor for the school's free milk program in grade 3. Every kid was given a little bottle of milk at playtime and the milk monitor got out 10 minutes earlier to set up the distribution. In grade four we also had turns to be the ink monitor. Each desk had ink well slots for the little containers that needed filling every session. We had progressed from HB pencils to a pen and nib writing instrument, with varying degrees of success. My first efforts were very messy and I was told that my work looked like a chook had scratched its way across the page. Lefthanded kids found it so much harder. Ask Heather; she's a Molly Duke. In fact, my sister Heather was forced to use her right hand, causing her great distress. This unfair practice was a common story for lefthanders.

I have less than fond memories of drawing classes. I was pretty hopeless and totally uninterested. I'd drawn a hill with a tree on each side of the page. I added a notice mounted on a post centre stage saying

'DO NOT THROW STONES AT THIS SIGN'. I liked it. The teacher said he thought my artwork was pointless and very silly, but I knew he was laughing on the inside. I liked to make people laugh and soon learned that it was a great way to calm stressful situations. Being a class clown also fended off the bullies.

We were encouraged by our school to collect empty metal (lead and tin) toothpaste tubes and the foil milk bottle caps for post-war recycling purposes.

Mainstream television came to Australia in 1956 in time for the Melbourne Olympic games. As a sevenyear- old kid, I had no idea what television was, but our school was about to show us all. I had a keen interest in film projection as Dad would often screen 16mm comedy and religious movies in the church hall. I was far more interested in the equipment than any religious content. I loved the Buster Keaton films and I knew how to thread up a 16mm Bell and Howell just from watching the projectionist.

Television came to my classroom in 1955. That's pretty amazing given that TV commenced a year later, but it was all done with bells and mirrors. The bell was the famous Bell and Howell 16mm projector and the mirror facilitated rear projection onto the small box that looked like a television set. I was not fooled or impressed. The noise of the projector was over-riding the audio and the image was so small compared to the great big movie screen we had in the church hall. Plus, our setup at the church hall was in colour, sometimes.

A huge aerial towering above the rooftops was needed to receive the TV signal in Echuca. This could cost more than the very expensive television receiver. Needless to say, we stayed with our beloved wireless for many years. The local electrical shop where Mum purchased our light bulbs and fuse wire stocked a couple of different brands of TV sets. (Mum was the handy-person in our house.)

The retailer displayed a TV set in the window and people would take their own deck chairs to set up on the footpath in the evening and experience television first hand. It was poor quality, snowy and unreliable.

Transmission commenced in the afternoon and shut down before midnight after playing the National Anthem. There were three Melbourne based stations on air, 7, 9 and 2.

Echuca in the mid-1950s was a typical, larger country town on the Murray River. The Astoria Café in Hare Street was just so posh to us. I don't ever remember having a meal there or at any other café for that matter. We simply didn't eat out with the notable exception of churchy functions, where the women were asked to 'bring a plate'. Next door to the Astoria was a toyshop. In the window was a red, wind-up speedboat that I admired every time I wandered past. It was about eight shillings and my funds didn't run to that sort of money. I was happy just to admire it through the glass. When I turned eight, my only lefthanded sister (irrelevant fact) Heather, presented me with that red wind-up speedboat. Oh joy!

We occasionally drove down to Melbourne for some functions Dad needed to attend and a couple of times Mum took me to Coles cafeteria #200 for lunch. My first real café-bought meals. I've loved ham and pickle sandwiches made with fresh white bread ever since. Back at Percy Street we kept a few chooks and a big red rooster, named Charlie. The girls had turns to feed the kitchen scraps to the birds but Roie couldn't quite grasp the double gate system. On one occasion Charlie got out and chased twelve-year-old Roie up Percy Street and back again before she locked herself in the pen for safety. She was rescued after a good deal of screaming out for help. Charlie had to go eventually, along with the other chooks.

Shirley cleaned up and converted the old chook house to her secret club. She installed a large sign on the door that shouted 'SECRET CLUB'. She was the undisputed CEO and Margie was 2 I.C. This boy was not granted membership. After all it was a secret club, so I formed my own, one boy, secret club under the roof of the car garage.

The girls liked to jump off the old garden shed roof sometimes with an old umbrella as a parachute.

Crystal Sets

My grade three teacher, Mr Mackenzie, a Scotsman, had been a signals operator in the army. He started an after-school class to teach kids how to make a crystal radio set. I jumped at this opportunity, along withabout four of my schoolmates. Exercising his strong Scottish bra bricht accent, he taught us how to wind coils, set up a cat's whisker and use a soldering iron. I rigged up a huge aerial across the house roof to the shed roof then down into the sleep-out. My first crystal set could pick up 3SR Shepparton and 2QN Deniliquin on a clear night. I remember listening to radio plays like 'The Shadow' and 'D24', featuring the spooky voiced Roland Strong. These programs scared the crap out of me, especially on a cold night with the louvre windows rattling to every breath of wind.

I really wanted my own soldering iron after this great crystal set making experience. Dad agreed. He arranged to get me an electric soldering iron, but it was way too big for my purpose. It was more suited to a plumber. Talk about using a hammer to crack a walnut! I never told him that little fact. I was so grateful and still able to use it for my little projects.

For my next birthday he presented me with a multi-meter direct from my wish list. I could now measure voltage, current flow and resistance/continuity. What boy wouldn't want to be able to do that?

Radio (wireless communication) was instrumental in framing my life. I have my radio on as I write and I'm listening to 3CR Saturday Jazz as I have for many, many years.

2QN Echuca

The Deniliquin based station had a studio in Echuca with a double glazed window facing High Street. After school, I could actually watch a live radio program go to air. The afternoon show featured a beautifully spoken announcer playing vinyl records and station announcements on a cartridge tape unit. The announcer was so animated in his presentation. I knew about good diction and voice control from my father's fine delivery techniques.

After watching this fellow through the glass for weeks, he invited me into the studio to sit quietly, and observe. How wonderful this was. I felt the hairs on the back of my seven-year-old neck stand to attention. The time calls were made to a real four-note xylophone on the presenter's desk The big RCA spring-mounted ribbon microphone added that theatrical touch. I absolutely loved my first studio experience and it's still with me.

Sunday School Concerts

The old wooden church hall next to our house was falling into disrepair. Dad set up a fund to finance its replacement with a modern, brick building complete with indoor toilets. One fund-raising idea came in the form of a series of Sunday school concerts with students being offered prizes for selling the most tickets.

At a price of a couple of shillings going to a very worthwhile cause, I decided to do the hard yards. I would go up and down the main streets offering this once in a lifetime entertainment extravaganza to total strangers. Many bought tickets just to get rid of me. I sold far more tickets than we had seats in the hall.

The audience was mainly made up from the Sunday school families anyway. Why would anyone else want to attend? The system worked and Dad was a very successful executive producer. He achieved additional financial support and the new hall was opened in March 1957.

The indoor toilets were labeled "GENTLEMEN" and "LADIES POWDER ROOM". I remember asking Mum what a powder room was. I did take a sneak look one day, and it was just a toilet.

The Helicopter Hoover

My interest in building crystal sets, followed on to many things mechanical or electrical. I loved pulling apart old alarm clocks and then trying to put them back together again. I usually failed this second stage. I remember finding an old Electrolux vacuum cleaner that someone had thrown out. I pulled it apart to find that the motor still worked. It had a large fan blade to create the air movement for suction. I reversed this fan and modified the mountings to create a helicopter type machine. I fashioned some sort of take-off stand from bits and pieces of junk and borrowed an extension power lead from the church hall. Once plugged into a power point, I stood clear and counted down. 5. 4. 3. 2. 1. Power on. The machine shot upwards and sideways, busted the extension lead and blew the main power fuse and landed with a huge thud.

Mum always fixed the fuses. She had no idea what caused this incident and I kept the secret to myself.

Mum had lots of tricks up her sleeve. She just knew how to keep the family functioning when Dad wasn't so well. With five kids to feed and clothe on a very limited income, she performed miracles. As with all young kids, I had the odd sick-day off school. Mum had a Kellogg's Corn Flakes box filled with lots of bits and pieces of things to do. Things to lace, colour match and games to play. All freebies. 'You don't need to buy this stuff'', she'd say. It was worth taking a sickie just to have the Kellogg's box. On my sixtieth birthday, my sisters reproduced this wonderful treasure filled box. I plan to pass it on to my grandchildren just as soon as I've finished with it.

My first business

Pocket money was pretty scarce and I felt that I really needed to generate my own. The local butcher shops used newspaper for the outer wrapping of their produce. One sheet of butcher's paper to three sheets of recycled newsprint. The going price for used, flat packed newspaper was two pence per pound. I set up a collection round by door knocking and asking if I could take away any old newspapers. There were no recycling services as such, so I could do the householder a favour.

I had my homemade billy-cart that I had built under instruction from Dad's friend, Mr Laurie. I replaced the driver's seat with a flat bit piece of wood to transport newspaper. There were three butchers in town who would buy paper from me. I could earn four or five shillings on a Saturday morning if I set out early enough. There was another client in Echuca East, but was a heck of a long way for me to pull the newspaper delivery cart. On the way home from my regular round I would call in at the post office and check for pennies under the scales. Bulked up people could not always get down to retrieve dropped pennies that rolled under the massive silver scales. I could, and I had a special flat stick to assist with the recovery. This usually yielded 4 or 5 pennies per week.

Lord's Newsagency

Here's a business opportunity if ever I saw one.

The early morning paper delivery boys were raking in a steady income from a couple of hours' effort, six days a week. Staff turnover was pretty high, as it was hard work for a young kid. Needless to say, the older boys lasted longer. They used a homemade hessian bag, slung across the bicycle's bar to transport the daily newspapers. I gave it a go for a few months but when the bag was full of papers, on a cold, wet morning, I could hardly pedal my bike. The Age newspaper was a broad sheet paper, very big on Wednesdays and bigger still on Saturdays. We also had the Argus, Melbourne Sun News Pictorial and the dishonestly named The Truth newspaper once a week. The bigger, older boys got the best rounds and I think this workplace was my first contact with a real bully. I wasn't equipped to handle such behaviour and found it best to make myself scarce.

The boss, Mr Lord, was a fine man and the local Justice of the Peace. His son, John, played football for Melbourne (#4), in the VFL. That was a big deal for me. Mr Lord offered me a job selling football records for the local footy competition. He thought that might be more suitable than the paper round and I could keep up my butcher's newspaper run.

Footy Records

Echuca football club (The Mighty Grasshoppers), played in the Bendigo league. The Footy Record listed the players' numbers, statistics and footy gossip. The Record was an essential tool for every serious supporter.

The game-day players list had columns to pencil in the scores from individual players as the game progressed. Competition to sell the booklets at the ground was fierce. Dad suggested that I could sell pencils with the footy record. Now, that's value adding. Lord's Newsagency also sold pencils. I asked Mr Lord for a bulk price on the 2 HB variety. So now, I have a box of 24 pencils, but this was adding to my overheads. These were full-length pencils and they didn't need to be. I borrowed a hacksaw and cut each pencil into three lengths. Now I have 72 pencils. I figured that if I add 2d for the package of footy record with pencil, that's 11d. Most customers will hand over one shilling (12 pence) leaving only one penny as change. Pennies were big, heavy and far better in my pocket, than in my customers'. The system worked perfectly.

Next season, most kids were selling pencils, too. I should have gone into pencil wholesaling. Even in the mid-1950s business was fiercely competitive.

Radio Station 2QN broadcast the football games from the Echuca oval.

After selling out of footy records stock, I'd make my way up to the grandstand front corner where two commentators would call the game on live to air. Once they'd got to know me, sometimes they would give me a set of cans (headphones) to listen to the broadcast. I just loved every minute. Radio was becoming my connection with the real world.

Here's something that caused me great discomfort.

In March 1959 The Billy Graham circus came to town. Billy Graham was a charismatic, fast talking American evangelist. Billy Graham was a business. Whilst he was touring the World telling others how to live their lives, his own deserted family was in crisis. Protestant churches around Victoria were recruited to support his massive crusade program. Our little Methodist church in Echuca was totally taken in with the frenetic 'Billy Graham' bug.

Graham's Melbourne crusade planned to deliver thousands of good people to repent, and give their lives to Christ. The rally was set for 15 March at the Melbourne Cricket Ground. The main event boasted the biggest ever crowd at the hallowed turf. Well over one hundred and fifteen thousand people attended and our little church sent a number of buses up to town. I was on one of them. The atmosphere was electric.

The warm-up artists were well polished and knew all the techniques to whip the audience into a hypnotic frenzy before the great man took the stage. The Southern Baptist big man beefed out his message and basically said that if you don't give your life to Christ tonight, you are doomed. "You had better do as I say, not as I do" was the key message. He sure put the frighteners on me. I was scared stiff. When the call came to come forward, my mate nudged me and said, 'We'd better go'. I walked down the aisle to the waiting volunteer counsellors, and was given some propaganda to read and follow. I was totally coerced into 'going forward'. There was no effective follow up. To this day I wish I had not made this move. Kids don't need this man-made nonsense. If my father was alive today, I'm sure he would agree that the Billy Graham experiment was a huge mistake. Donald Trump surely picked up many mass-marketing tips from such showmen. They sell the sizzle not the sausage. It's all in the flashy showmanship.

The Bye family years in Echuca were pretty darn good. Seven people in a little two, plus one, bedroom house. No TV, one wireless, one piano. I don't ever remember a cross word spoken. How many people can say that?

My oldest sister, or should that be, eldest sister, Shirley, met a young man at church. His name was, and still is, Geoff, and his father sang in the choir at church. I always thought old Mr Harvey sang in the choir to escape the other church duties. Anyway, Geoff took a liking to my sister. He had a farming job out in Bamawm

Extension, about 12 miles out of town, but he still rode his bicycle into town every weekend. Why so? I think we all knew. My three other sisters used to spy on Geoff and Shirl's intimate moments from behind the grapevine. When the big pash arrived, they would sing, 'Wedding bells will ring so merrily, every time Shirley's kissing Geoff-er-ree'. Clearly, music was in our DNA.

As a footnote.

Shirl and Geoff are still together and have four great kids, 65 grand children and about 150* great, great grand kids. This may be a slight exaggeration.

*Again, I'm not in a position to fact check this.

The Secret Club (no boys allowed)

Parachuting off the garden shed

6 - SUMMER HOLIDAYS

Again Dad's heart condition caused him to be bedridden for a number of months. In 1958 we had an extremely hot summer in Echuca. We had no cooling system. A canvas tarpaulin was set up to shade the bedroom window and we had a roster to keep it wet on very hot days. This was a proven, time-honoured, air-conditioning system that worked well. At the time, Dad had a huge tank of oxygen at his bedside, which really spooked me. I wondered how long he would live and what happens if he doesn't. What do we all do then and what about our poor Mum?

We all had our jobs to do, but it was Mum who kept the household running smoothly. There wasn't much that this little lady couldn't do. I know I'm repeating myself but it's a fact worth clearly driving home.

It was school holidays, having just turned 10, I was sent to the Tomlinson family farm for a week. I'd never been away from home and I was terrified. They had a ramshackle farm with chooks, goats and ducks, all wandering free. They also ran the local manual telephone exchange. Anytime day or night, when the bell rang, Mrs Tomlinson would go out to the shed where the telephone exchange was located and make the manual connection. I'm sure the odd call would be listened into. On completion, the caller would ring off, and the cords were removed. I loved seeing the exchange in action but I was so homesick.

Our home number was Echuca 137 and our old, black bakelite phone had a magneto handle in the centre.

To make a call, which I was not allowed to do, you would lift the handset and wind the handle. The operator would ask what number you wanted, and manually connect the call. To finish, wind the handle again and ring off.

Sometimes I think my older sisters received occasional calls from boys they knew. I didn't receive any calls!

After the school holidays Dad was again on his feet and I was back at school. My parents thought Cubs (Boy Scouts) would be a good experience for me in my new setting. I was required to turn up at the scout hall once a week after school. I remember that I didn't have the full uniform but I had a pre-loved cap, a scarf and a woggle. I was promised a full cub uniform once I'd passed the 6-week trial period. I didn't like tying knots, bush tucker or dib-dob-dibbing. The only highlight I remember was being taken out with the cub scouts to see the first Russian satellite, Sputnik, pass overhead in 1957. I never got the uniform. I wasn't much of a team player, and I didn't need another set of rules to follow.

7 - SANDRINGHAM

Heather, Roie and I didn't particularly want to move to the big city. I don't think our mother did either. For me it meant leaving friends and, furthermore, our free and easy country lifestyle. My two eldest sisters were already living in Melbourne, training to be nurses. Heather had finished high school and Roie and I were enrolled at Highett High School. Our new school had the unlikely motto, 'Forward and Upward'. It opened in 1956 so we were true Olympians, according to the school song. I had no idea how a big city high school worked.

Methodist ministers were moved about every seven years in an attempt to refresh the system. Bank managers, police officers and many other public servants were on even shorter relocation cycles. It's not that easy on the other family members, but that's how it was. One of the very few good things about

Highett High School was that it had a tuck shop, which served mainly junk food. I'd never seen a pineapple doughnut. I was allowed to buy my lunch once a fortnight and always squeezed in this newfound delicacy.

One truly awful facet was that my father was taking religious instruction classes at the school, and he rocked up once or twice a week, complete with his clerical collar. This archaic 19th century religious icon made him stand out and again I was constantly asked why my father had his shirt back to front. (In later years thankfully he ditched the collar.) My new school was far too regimented for my liking. Different classes were conducted in different rooms with specialist teachers. I hated that; lugging heavy books around the prefabricated classrooms. My mathematics teacher wore a gown and a frown, as did the headmaster. To top things off, this new lifestyle included homework. I was far too busy for this unwelcome imposition on my recreational activities.

I had a crystal set in my bedroom and I could now get so many new radio stations. Later, I got my hands on a wireless set. I bought a pair of army surplus headphones and connected them to the wireless. I could now listen in without anyone else hearing any sounds leaking out from my bedroom. I thought wearing cans (headphones) was really cool, even though no one saw me.

Heather joined the workforce and I think she had a boyfriend, too. Margie had a one year cadetship at the Eye & Ear hospital in Melbourne prior to training as a nurse at Prince Henry's Hospital. Her boyfriend, Alan Lacey, whom she later married, played amateur football. I was impressed. Shirley was studying nursing at Bendigo Base Hospital. She had her childhood sweetheart, Geoff, who also had been a pretty handy footballer, so I'm told. My two eldest sisters were hardly ever home. I wonder why.

Dad announced that we were getting a television set, and he would decide when it could be 'operated' and what programs made for suitable viewing. That rigid censorship plan soon eased. I liked to watch shows such as Sea Hunt, Whirly Birds and, of course, Skippy, The Bush Kangaroo. Dad and mum liked the quiz show 'Pick-a-box' with Bob and Dolly Dyer at 7 pm weeknights. Dad never missed his weekly serve of 'Meet the Press', an hour of political and current affairs talking heads.

Dinner was fairly formal at our house in the fifties and sixties. Certainly no television and the kitchen wireless turned off. After dinner Dad often had church affairs to attend. The rest of us had washing up duties and then Roie and I were supposed to attend to our homework. I have no idea what she did, but I knew 'Jazz as you like it' was on 3XY at 7:30. That was my type of music and with my headphones on, no one knew it was jazz before homework.

I loved playing around with radio sets and the public address systems that we had in the church and the church hall. We lived next door, so I could pop in anytime. I saved up my pocket money to buy the monthly magazine, Radio and Hobbies. I had the use of a little shed at Sandringham, and it was here that I set up a little workshop to fix up old radios. I became a competent 'valve jockey'. Most radios used a similar set of glass valves and by swapping kind for kind, most common problems were solved and the dead old wireless would burst back into life. There was always someone at the church to help me out with tricky issues and a never-ending supply of old sets to raid for parts. As I became more experienced, I put up a huge 'RADIO REPAIRS' sign on the shed roof. This could be seen from the church car park and the tennis courts. At 14, I had a neat little business going.

The church committee bought a new Victa lawnmower and they had a roster for whoever was to mow the little lawn in front of the church each fortnight. I asked if I could do this in return for mowing other lawns. I managed to get a little mowing round set up, and charged four shillings a pop. I bought the petrol and used the church mower. This little earner worked quite well for a few months until one of the church hierarchy complained. A few months later the same stuffy deacon complained about the sign advertising my other enterprise. The sign was on church property as was our house, and my workshop. The sign had to come down and the radio repairs business petered out. I needed to replace this income.

The Total Service Station on Bay Road, Sandringham, was looking for a bowser boy, and that was me. I worked a couple of hours after school and Saturday mornings. One of the part owners was a little round man named Nugget McConechy.

Nugget was always building and repairing stock racing cars in the workshop. When the driveway wasn't busy, he'd get me to help with little chores and always explained exactly what he was doing. He taught me arc welding. Nugget McConechy lost his life years later in a crash at the Daylesford stock car race track.

Nugget had a brother, Joe, whom I met at the service station a few times. When I told him I was having music lessons at Sutton's Music Store, Joe went on to tell me he was a bass player. He was a very modest man, but it turned out that he played in many famous Australian jazz bands. Joe was the first jazz musician I ever met, along with Norm Hodges, who bought his petrol from the service station for his motor mowers. Norm had a mowing round to supplement his modest earnings as a jazz musician. He was Allan Browne's drum teacher in later times. Allan became the leader of the Red Onions Jazz Band.

Joe was a highly respected musician who died, sadly, in August 2019, just shy of his 84th birthday.

8 - THE PRE-BAND YEARS

From about the age of twelve I dreamt of playing in a real jazz band. I'm talking about a seven-piece traditional jazz band. The front line would be clarinet and trombone with me in the middle, playing trumpet. The rhythm section would feature, piano, bass (or tuba), banjo and drums.

I needed a plan.

We'd just moved from Echuca to Sandringham.

The local town council had a brass band, always looking for new young players. A school friend's father played trombone in the Sandringham Brass Band, and he arranged an interview for me. I didn't have an instrument and, with only a few piano lessons to my musical education, I had no idea about brass instruments. The brass band guys were so helpful and after a few information meetings, I was lent a cornet and lessons began. It was an after school, weekly commitment, with plenty of homework. This is exactly what I wanted...this was my idea of homework despite the torture I was about to inflict upon anyone within earshot.

At the Sandringham Methodist we had the Rampling Family Band that seemed to play at every social occasion. Mrs Rampling was a jolly, generously rounded pianist while her little jockey sized husband played drums. I took piano lessons with Mrs Rampling. She told me jazz players must have an understanding of chord structures, and she was spot on. The Methodists frowned on dancing until late into 1950s-early sixties. Maybe some folk may confuse dancing with making love standing up. We didn't have dances in our church hall. I never saw my parents dance. I doubt they ever did.

Dad was big on Outreach. He knew how to connect and was an impressive communicator. Sunday night church services in winter were suffering from dwindling attendances.

Dad, together with his two close church friends, decided to run a free, after church coffee lounge in the church hall.

Bert Perkin, whose son, Graham, was the editor of the Age newspaper, was the head chef. He knew how to make raisin toast. Heck Oakley, whose sons were first grade football players, knew all the promotion techniques of the day. Dennis Oakley played for Sandringham in the VFA and Ross, who was my Sunday school teacher at one stage, went on to play for St Kilda. Ross later became president of the Victorian Football League. The Oakley brothers always helped with the set up.

Dennis was a policeman and later became an ordained Methodist minister. Dad was his mentor at one stage.

In the winter of 1962 'Bert's Bistro' opened every Sunday evening at 8 pm.

Dimly lit, with low tables and plenty of cushions.

The simple menu featured Nescafe coffee, hot chocolate, crumpets and raisin toast.

Hardly a bistro, but a real hit with teenagers.

There was NO DANCING.

Here's the really exciting part for me.

'Bert's Bistro' had a house band and a PA system that I was allowed to help set up.

The band was very much a scratch band, led by John Rhodes on alto sax. He had plenty of muso mates who were keen to sit in, all unpaid. John later lent me a spare alto sax and gave me a number of lessons.

My first recognisable ballad was Moon River. It wasn't easy listening.

I kept on with trumpet lessons, but not the sax.

At 14, I wasn't ready to sit in at 'Bert's Bistro', but I loved setting up the stage lighting and audio system.

I fear that Dad copped an unfair amount of criticism from a few 'locked in' old Methodist fundamentalists for running this project on the 'Lord's Day'.

Bert's Bistro

9 - FORMING MY FIRST BAND

I always had my birthday at the start of the New Year. 1963 was no exception, and on January 4th, I turned 15.

By now I'd handed back the brass band cornet and I had my own student standard trumpet. When school recommenced in February I met Brian Cadd, who was two years ahead of me at school. Brian had moved over from Tasmania and played piano, clearly having had some classical training.

Lunchtimes would find him in the music room at Highett High. His showpiece was 'Fur Elise'. He'd play the first 12 bars as written, then stomp his foot, and rock it up. The girls loved it. He sure could play and I needed a strong piano to get my project off the ground. We got together after school and on weekends and had a blow. Another student, Mark Davey in a higher class, had a trombone. I needed a trombone player, which he really wasn't...yet. He did have the necessary instrument and with a little encouragement, he joined up, and agreed to have private lessons on this fine piece of plumbing.

I knew another kid, younger than me, who was taking drumming lessons with the legendary Billy Hyde.

Rod Weaver was very good at what he did, even though he only wanted to play rock music. He had a mate, Doug Van Daman, who played guitar and owned a banjo. Now, we were getting somewhere. The rhythm section was almost in place, but the front line was missing a reed player, preferably a clarinet player. I also needed a bass or tuba player in the rhythm section, but I will come back to that challenge. I made a list of tunes to get the band started. I still have my notes outlining our initial repertoire.

We're leading off with the absolute standards.
- When the Saints Go Marching In
- Bill Bailey
- Apex Blues
- Tin Roof Blues (much the same as above, but backwards)
- South
- Joshua Hit the Bottle at Jericho (That gets a laugh)
- Beale Street Blues (There's the band's name...Beale Street.)

I bought a music book titled '1001 Jazz Standards' at Clemen's music store in Russell Street, Melbourne. I wrote out the chords to the above tunes, and rehearsals began in the church hall or sometimes at Brian's place in Sandringham. The early band practice sessions did not require Rod on his noisy drum kit. For myself and Mark (trom) I chose the easy keys for us newbie brass players (Bb F Eb). Brian hated these keys at first. He had never played trad jazz and this soon became pretty clear.

The Beale Street Jazz Band was coming together right at the time when Melbourne was enjoying a huge jazz revival although rock 'n' roll was as strong as ever.

Dance and jazz clubs were popping up right across town.

There were a few jazz programs on the radio and, amazingly, one of the most popular was on country radio, 3CS in Colac (a small regional country town) with John Thompson heading the volunteer presenters. This Saturday morning jazz show had a huge Melbourne jazz fan-based audience. I knew if we could get our new gig plugged here it would be invaluable. John was a terrific support for my project and turned up at Beale Street many times. He told me he'd never worked with a fifteen-year-old jazz dance promoter before.

In the early sixties the big decision; "Are you a Jazza or a Rocker?"

If you're a Jazza, get yourself a duffle coat, jeans and desert boots. Now say 'cool, man and snap your fingers'. Make sure your hair is scruffy and not clean and shiny.

Rockers, you guys need to look tough, cut your hair short, plenty of Brylcreem and wear a white T-shirt with a black cardigan. Tight black jeans and boots as part of the uniform.

Now say, "What are you lookin' at?"

I told my fellow band members that I would manage the band and find paid work, once we had twenty-five or thirty well-rehearsed tunes on our play list.

I knew that the only way I could keep the band together was to set a clear plan to get paying gigs, even if I had to start my own jazz club/dance.

I still needed a clarinet and a tuba player, but I figured that the current line up needed a lot of work and rehearsals are easier with fewer players. At every band practice, we first played the tunes we knew and then added two or three more.

Brian and I would often meet between rehearsals to set the tune list. At the church hall practice sessions we were attracting quite a few kids just to watch us rehearse. I encouraged this as it created a good vibe and the guys tried harder even with this micro-audience. We were improving, albeit from a low base.

We are now a band of five and I'd heard that someone wanted a band to play a few numbers at an 18th birthday party. I followed up the lead and we had our first booking in April 1963. We were paid two pounds, which divided by five, amounted to eight shillings each.

We had the taste for success but needed two more players. I heard around the traps that Allan Roberts, from nearby Black Rock, was playing tuba and he knew a pretty good clarinet player, Russell Wild. I approached these guys and asked them to join my band. They weren't terribly keen at first.

They both had some band experience, but they were not getting any paid gigs. I had to think on my feet to get these guys interested. I laid out my business plan for the Beale Street Jazz Band.

Once we achieved a well-rehearsed repertoire that could sustain an evening's program, I was going to hire a public hall, print posters, and run our own Beale Street Jazz Club. They were impressed. I was impressed. I did most of my thinking out aloud. They were in. I had a real keen, seven-piece jazz band.

The first band rehearsal was not good. I had checked that the church hall was free and could be used for our purpose.

Rod set up his shiny new student drum kit while Brian checked that the old piano hadn't drifted too far out of tune. Just as the other guys tuned to the piano, the sounds of a ping-pong game filled the hall. I hadn't been told that the table tennis club was meeting in the smaller, adjacent room. They informed me that they would only be playing for another half hour or so.

Doug, our banjo player (read "owner") had only brought his electric guitar and amp along. He forgot about the banjo.

Russell Wild hadn't turned up, so no clarinet for this session. I had the first seven or eight tunes set in order of ease of playing, with the chords written out, ready to go. We kicked off The Beale St Jazz Band with the 'Saints'.

Brian played four bars in and off we went. Trumpet and trombone almost in unison in the front line, and Brian playing piano like a front-line instrument. The rhythm section was totally drowned out by our young, enthusiastic, wannabe, rock drummer. Electric guitar and tuba seemed a total mismatch.

We seemed to have invented the sound of soup!

We regrouped after a few attempts at playing 'When The Saints Go Marching In'. The drums and guitar had to come down by 20db and we needed to give each other a little space, musically. The trombone needed to vary from playing in unison with the trumpet. A touch of harmony would have improved the overall sound!

The ping-pong noises stopped and the table tennis guys came in to see what the racket was about.

Again we had an audience.

"Let's move on to Bill Bailey", I suggested. "This time Brian and I will play it through with just Rod playing hi-hat. That way we can all hear what the tune really is. Next run through, trombone and tuba join in and we'll go again adding guitar". We were sounding better with each session, but the audience left anyway.

We agreed to meet same time, next week. Doug agreed to bring his banjo and leave his guitar and amp in the shed. Rod was to play a scaled down drum kit. This turned out to be a much better session despite

Russ not turning up, again. I had to follow up as to why he didn't show up for the second session. It turned out he had a gig with another band, but hadn't been paid as promised, so he was still happy to play gigs with us. He still wouldn't commit to band practices at that stage. I needed him more than he needed us. I knew of no other clarinet players I could call on at that time.

We continued to grow our list and improve with each session.

10 - BEALE STREET JAZZ CLUB

Three months after forming the band I totally understood that the only way we could get a regular paying gig was for me to hire a hall, spread the good news and get started with the Beale Street Jazz Club. The church hall was not an option, for so many reasons, not the least being the anti-dancing mentality.

The best public hall I could find was in nearby Black Rock. At 15 years of age it was difficult at first to be taken seriously as a potential, regular hirer of a community hall. Somehow I managed to secure an agreement to hire the hall on a fortnightly basis, initially for three months. The hall was ideally located, with capacity for 250+ dancers. It featured a big stage, complete with an almost-in-tune upright piano. We were to start at 7:30 pm and finish at 10:30 pm sharp. We were obliged to play the national anthem (God Save The Queen) after our final tune.

I set the opening date as Saturday May 18th 1963.

I arranged with a local printer to have 250 flyers printed and a number of free one-for-one passes. I had to pay the printer in advance, as he wasn't sure how this kid would be able to put such an ambitious show together. I had some financial reserves from my radio repair business and working as a bowser boy at the Total petrol station.

Once the guys in the band became aware that the project was really happening, the enthusiasm escalated to a whole new level. Even Russell Wild turned up to rehearsals. I also managed to get Allan Roberts to officially join the band on tuba. We now had a complete seven-piece traditional jazz band.

About ten days before opening night I arranged to launch the publicity campaign. The advertising budget was extremely tight. We made up a bucket of paste using wheat starch and headed off to plaster the leaflets on poles near the local secondary schools. We put them everywhere we thought our target audience would see them. We gave out the one-for-one passes mainly to girls as they always went to dances in groups. The one free, one paying offer was limited to the May 18th event.

I did receive a little negative feedback regarding the leaflets. I felt that they were not big enough to cause any major problems, as the glue would break down with the first rain shower.

A few cranky people complained. The council must have given them my phone number. I can only imagine their confusion when the phone was answered with, "Good morning, Methodist manse, Sandringham".

Dad was pretty good about the whole project, not that I told him too much, at the time. On the big day, I rode my bike to the Black Rock council office and collected the hall keys at 10 am, as arranged. A few of the band members came down before the final rehearsal, to check out the venue. In the kitchen there was a big old banner reading, 'BE REALLY REFRESHED WITH COKE'.

With a little modification, it soon read 'BEALE ST'.

Our afternoon rehearsal brought out the nerves. Russell and Mark were sparring with each other and Rod was still playing far too loud. The empty hall was like an echo chamber, but I told the guys that with the hall full of people, the acoustics would dramatically improve. This was our opportunity to play to an audience of our age range, have fun and earn a few quid. I had arranged for a few trusted friends to attend to the door and I had one big guy, who had a black belt in Judo, stand and keep watch. The entrance price was five shillings and I had a good supply of change in the cash drawer.

I was a little concerned that if we didn't draw a reasonable number of paying patrons, I was going to be well out of pocket, and the band could fold.

At 7 the doors opened. A crowd of teenagers had lined up to pay their five shillings or use the special opening offer card. Thankfully, most paid the five bob.

The crowd outside waiting to get in was growing by the minute. By 7:20 the hall was at capacity, maybe 400 kids, far more girls than guys. That was good; very good.

We needed to start playing a little earlier than scheduled to settle things down. We kicked the show off with the 'Saints'. We were by far the youngest band playing traditional jazz at the time, only Russel Wild was old enough to have a driver's licence. The young audience loved our enthusiastic performance. Our repertoire was running out well before the last set was completed, so I announced that we'd had a few requests to play a few favourites again. That stretched out our play list until it was time for the national anthem.

We were much better than we sounded! (Thanks Richard for that line.) Beale Street Jazz Club was up and running and displayed a hurriedly made 'FULL HOUSE' sign out front. The band's line-up changed from time to time due to the availability of our young members. This gave me the opportunity to build a list of reserve players, which became invaluable for future projects. Jeff Hale replaced Rod on drums, and his friend, Allan Mittleman, played banjo in place of Doug. I felt that I also needed to feature a young female singer to balance the audience appeal mix. We came across a young, keen singer named Lyn Angus, who looked the part, so she was featured on a few songs throughout the show.

In between the now well-established fortnightly gig, I actively looked out for other opportunities including private parties and school functions. We also played in a few coffee lounges, and on several gigs on the back of a truck to promote local fetes and shopping centre promotions including a gig in the carpark at Chadstone shopping centre.

The band was now earning very good money, and was keen to improve. However, as Beale St became more popular it also became more and more difficult to control the growing audience. Over the next few months the crowds increased and the situation became volatile. We were attracting a group of guys who just wanted to fight and disrupt the show. On some nights we played the national anthem early just to control the brawling morons. This commenced with a dramatic drumroll; everyone was expected to stand to attention in respect. That stopped the fighting! Immediately, the house fluorescent lights were turned on, and the show was over.

The more bouncers I employed, the tougher it became.

Beale Street Jazz club closed in October 1963.

The guys in the band weren't particularly good mates and the standard of musicianship varied greatly. We were a novelty, young, discombobulated band that had run its race.

Brian was a good piano player but not a great jazz musician by any means. As a trumpet player, I was a good organiser and manager. Russ had a nice tone on the clarinet, but Mark said he played like a snake charmer. Russ said Mark's trombone sounded like it had a sock in it.

The Beale Street Jazz Band era was over.

Sadly Russell Wild was killed in a car crash on his way home from a gig. Allan Roberts, our tuba player, was conscripted to the Vietnam War misadventure and did not return.

Brian Cadd was a very skinny kid, at the time. He had a short-term girl friend who nicknamed him 'spindles'. He went on to great heights in the Rock and Roll music industry as a singer/songwriter/ keyboardist in such bands as The Groop, Axiom and his Bootleg Family Band. He knew how to play a room. Still does.

Allan Mittleman achieved fame as an artist and art teacher. He was the subject of a winning Archibald portrait prize. I'm convinced his being a member of the Beale St Jazz Band was influential. He still dines out on this fact to this very day (maybe not).

First rehearsal with Brian Cadd

11 - BAY CITY JAZZ BAND

My next band needed to be far more polished and professional to survive in a very crowded jazz scene. Melbourne had some great bands attracting huge audiences. Bands like The Red Onions, The Yarra Yarra New Orleans Jazz Band and John Hawes Jazz Band. There were numerous bands with older, far more experienced musicians playing all around town. Equally, there was a number of bands scratching to get the odd, poorly paid gig. I wanted to surround myself with very good, young players and set the band up to play tunes the audiences wanted to hear. Most traditional bands around town were 'purists', playing what they wanted their audience to hear.

This was never my plan.

I had collected a list of possible players over the past months and, I knew that I could attract young musicians far above my own playing standard, providing the paying gigs were there. My plan was to have a very young band playing tunes the kids knew and loved, including popular hit songs that adapted easily to a traditional jazz setting. There were enough bands playing the complicated, purist stuff. I had no shame in turning the nose of the odd self-appointed jazz purists north.

I loved the San Francisco style of jazz as played by Turk Murphy's Bay City Jazz Band. What a great name. Melbourne is a bay city. I registered the business name 'Bay City' in 1963.

I didn't want to run any more gigs like Beale Street myself. That's a full time job on its own and I was still in form two at Highett High School.

I had a would-be-promoter contact me when he heard I was forming another band. He and his business partner were very keen to re-open a dance at the Black Rock Community Hall. This happened late in 1963 under the name 'Bullfight'. Rather a strange name, I thought, as it was the fights that closed Beale Street at the very same venue.

In late 1963 there were a few other possible gigs on the horizon so I needed to get cracking. I called around my contacts and had a suitable line-up within two weeks. I did receive a few knock-backs from guys who thought they were far too good to be in my band. That's fine; there were plenty of fine, young musos wanting to play in a successful, working band. I knew I was punching way above my weight musically, but I also knew how to manage a band. I grabbed at the chance to be the first band at Bullfight, and the date was set.

We rehearsed the tune list that I had prepared and we were set to go in a very short time. I was so fortunate to have the amazing Ian Clyne on piano, John Ellis on reeds, Ivan Cocking on trombone and his brother, Ian, on bass. John Reid joined on banjo and a much improved, young Rod Weaver completed the band on drums.

The guys who promoted Bullfight came from an advertising/marketing background and had good financial reserves.

The Bay City Jazz Band was booked for the opening sessions. The plan was to rotate a number of bands on a regular basis. We played the first two gigs there, after which the promoters put on a very professional group made up from session players from the Channel 9 TV band. The audience didn't relate to this band, at all. Next, The Yarra Yarra New Orleans band took to the stage with a very young Judy Jacques, who completely stole the show. What a drawcard she was to become for many years to follow.

We played a number of other gigs around the Brighton and Hampton area. I was always on the lookout for more work. Ian Clyne was a standout musician and a great guy to be around. It came as no surprise that he had other bands chasing his services. Incidentally, his father was a pharmacist and Ian was a reliable source of condoms for any band members who had the need. He supplied me with one, which I kept on standby in my wallet for two years. It actually wore a ring-shaped image into my leather wallet, which stayed with me for years to come. By the time I thought I may need the services of this little chap, it had disintegrated and only the ring remained intact. Disappointment all around.

Ian joined the Red Onions and later split away to form The Loved Ones, with Gerry Humphries and Kym Lynch. That band was hugely successful, yet somewhat short-lived.

TV Auditions

Around mid-1964, Melbourne television station GTV 9 featured a TV audition program on Saturday mornings, at 8 am, called Kevin Dennis New Faces. The program probably came from the hugely successful Radio Auditions talent show on Melbourne radio station The Greater 3UZ. Sadly, so many acts had ambitions far exceeding their talent, but it did make great listening!

The purpose of Kevin Dennis New Faces was 'to discover new talent for television'. The sponsor, Kevin Dennis, was a colourful, charismatic car dealer. There had never been a jazz band appear on KDNF.

The purist bands playing around town almost choked on their verbal tut-tutting at such commercialism. I welcomed it. Any publicity, as they say, is good publicity. The series winners were given a slot on Graham Kennedy's 'In Melbourne Tonight' show. Graham Kennedy, who once starred on radio 3UZ was now the undisputed King of Melbourne television in the sixties and seventies.

The Bay City Jazz Band now had a clear goal and a slightly changed line-up that was to remain stable for the next two years. New guys were Terry Villis banjo/guitar, Peter Wilson bass, Ray Evans drums, and the amazing Allan Zavod on piano. Again, I had a standout pianist. Allan went on to tour with Frank Zappa and the 'who's who' of jazz musicians world wide. However, in 1964-5 he was in my band and we remained friends until his death in 2016.

We appeared on New Faces in mid 1964 and went on to the finals of the series. We were described as a 'fresh-faced, exciting group of fine young musicians'.

I know, because I wrote that quote.

On the morning of the KDNF series grand final, we arrived at GTV 9, 22 Bendigo Street Richmond, at 7 am, ready to do our best to secure a spot on IMT. In the green room, I checked out the opposition, only to be mortified to see that we were up against, one Miss Olivia Newton-John. She was 16, and absolutely gorgeous and talented. (I was 16, but that's where similarity stopped.) Olivia screamed charisma.

The show's compere, Frank Wilson, mingled with the nervous contestants and tried to make everyone feel a little more relaxed. We'd been to makeup and had a good serving of pancake #9 applied to our faces. It was black and white television after all. Olivia had her own makeup people. My plan was now plan 'B'.

That was, come second. That would still secure us an appearance on In Melbourne Tonight, and that was the goal. We had our brand new band uniforms on and we gave a good, entertaining performance that ensured we achieved our goal. We came second.

We were to appear on IMT in one month's time.

In the meantime, I needed to look for paying gigs and that was a constant challenge.

I'd heard that 431 Jazz Club, at the nurse's home hall, 431 St Kilda Road Melbourne was struggling to maintain good audiences. The house band was the Geoff Hawes Jazz Band. The word was that they didn't appeal to the much younger patrons. Geoff's younger brother, John, had a very exciting band, but he wasn't going to go after his brother's gig. I would.

I approached the 431 management. I suggested that if we were given one booking for a Saturday night, and we packed the place out, the gig should be ours. After all, there was talk of 431 folding due to dwindling audiences and fierce competition from nearby Opus and Keyboard Jazz Clubs, which were attracting the older audiences (18+). We had our IMT booking coming up, so the date I suggested for our 431 trial was the Saturday after our IMT appearance.

The rules for appearing on Graham's flagship program were clearly set out by the producer, Bob Phillips.

Rehearsal time, makeup, dinner in the channel 9 canteen. No box unchecked. Do not approach the star of the show and do as directed. I was OK with all this, except I did need to speak to Mr Kennedy, re our 431 trial.

His dressing room was a caravan out past the props area. After our camera rehearsal, I strolled out through the props and knocked on his caravan door. This was a make or break decision and I had nothing to lose. He could tell me off, but there was no security, so I wasn't going to be tackled. I knocked again. He opened the flimsy caravan door and asked what the hell I wanted. He didn't invite me in, but he did listen to my plea. When I finished my presentation, he told me I was totally out of bounds. Ouch! Maybe I've blown it. 9:30 pm Monday night IMT, mid-September 1964 GTV 9

The 'In Melbourne Tonight' theme bursts out and we are live to air. The King arrives to a frenzy of applause. He goes through his opening set and then to a live commercial break, featuring his straight man,

Bert Newton. As this is going to air, my band is ushered on to the set ready to make our first ever IMT appearance. The tension is rising and I can see the guys are very nervous, all except Allan Zavod. He was so cool. I pointed to him..."follow his lead, guys".

Graham was back at his desk ready to introduce the band, but he breaks into a three-minute diatribe about how this kid turned up at his dressing room (caravan) to ask if he could promote a gig they had at 431 this Saturday night, at 8. He went on and on. The audience loved it, I loved it and 431 became part of my life for the next two years. 431 was well managed and a very safe venue for the well-heeled teenage audience it attracted. Again, we finished every gig with the national anthem. That's akin to the churchgoer's benediction.

We played on IMT many times between 1964 and 1966.

BAYCITY JAZZ GROUP NOW

VIEWERS who bombarded GTV9's switchboard after the Baycity Jazz Group had played on IMT last week have got their wishes—the youthful band has been signed for regular appearances.

Enthusiasm of viewers for the group was reminiscent of the old IMT days when phones rang hot and almost blew the Richmond telephone exchange night after night.

"It was a Graham Kennedy type response," a spokesman said.

More than 200 people phoned GTV9. Executives took only a few minutes at top level the next day to sign the group for regular performances.

And the seven members of the group — graduates from Kevin Dennis's Saturday morning TV show, New Faces — were just as surprised as GTV9 the night before when told they were wanted as permanents.

"Phew! What a windfall," exclaimed 16-year-old John Bye, leader of the seven young-man group. John, who is a student, plays the trumpet.

Other members are:

John Ellis, 18, painter, of Lower Templestowe, clarinet. Allan Zavod, 17, student, of Caulfield, piano. Ivan Cocking, 20, bank clerk, of Watsonia, trombone. Terry Villis, 18, student, of Dandenong, banjo. Ray Evans, 17, student, of Moorabbin, drummer. Steve Wilson, 21, trainee manager, of Sandringham, bass.

John Bye explained the group was the amalgamation of two jazz bands — The Northside and the original Baycity.

"We had a jam session together one night, thought it sounded pretty good and decided to team up," he added.

Page 30—TV WEEK—OCTOBER 10, 1964

GTV9 REGULARS

ONE appearance on IMT clinched a regular spot for them — the Baycity Jazz Band boys (left to right): John Ellis, Ivan Cocking, Allan Zavod, Ray Ellis, John Bye, Terry Villis and Steve Wilson.

The boys play trad jazz and "mainstream," a cross between trad and modern jazz.

12 - DOWNBEAT CONCERTS

Melbourne music shop owner and promoter, Bob Clemens, ran a series of jazz concerts between 1952 and 1968.

In the mid sixties the concerts were held in the Melbourne Town Hall and compered by Geoff Brooke of Radio 3KZ fame. Geoff was also a judge on Kevin Dennis New Faces at the time.

Adelaide jazz impresario, Kym Bonython, also promoted and compered a number of jazz concerts in the Melbourne Town Hall in conjunction with Bob Clemens.

In May 1964 we played our first Downbeat concert. We were the youngest band to play Downbeat and performed our twenty-minute set, first up. This concert also featured folk singer, Margaret Roadnight, in her first Downbeat appearance. She went on to become a very popular recording artist and is still active in the music scene.

The printed program listed the seven bands featured and the guest artists. Also on the program of the 84th Downbeat concert, was an ad for the forthcoming concert tour of Peter, Paul and Mary and the following teaser...

Also coming...a group named The Beatles in June.

I treasure this program and I'm so happy I still have my comprehensive scrapbook to assist in bringing these memories to life. The Bay City Jazz Band played at a number of Bob's town hall concerts over the next two years.

Downbeat Jazz Club

Clemens Music sponsored the Downbeat Jazz Club in a room above their store at 175 Russell Street. The entrance was via a rickety, outside set of stairs that more resembled a fire escape. The doorman was a very well rounded man aptly named 'Johnny Icecream'.

The Downbeat Jazz Club featured different bands from Wednesday to Sunday nights. It was advertised as six shillings and sixpence (6/6) at the door...modern food and coffee bar.

'NO CHARACTERS ADMITTED'

I suggested to Bob Clemens that we should try a special kids' jazz club experience during the school holidays in September 1964. My band had quite a following of high school aged kids and I thought this might just work.

We played six gigs over two weeks, Wednesday to Friday, 12:00 noon to 3 pm over the two-week break. At three shillings a pop, it was hugely successful. Subsequently, the band managed to secure a regular Wednesday night gig at Downbeat Jazz Club in 1964. The payment was a share of the door takings. In Melbourne's unreliable weather conditions, that could be pretty slim pickings on some nights.

To my horror, on our third Wednesday night gig I noticed my Highett High School maths teacher bopping around.

He took a second, and third, look at me:

Oh! This spells trouble!

I felt a little downbeat ... literally.

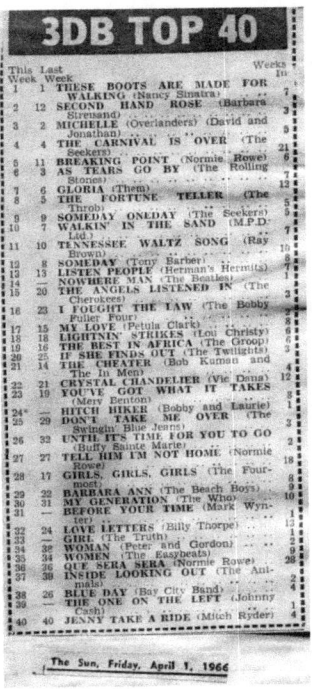

DOWNBEAT
presented by BOB CLEMENS

JAZZ at the... TOWN HALL
Continuous Jazz Concert

MISS LEONORE SOMERSET

MORWELL'S BASIN STREET SIX and **JOAN CLARKE**

SNY CHAMBERS BAYSIDE JAZZ BAND

ALLAN TURNBULL TRIO and LYN SLY	The Barnacle Bill Boys **RED ONION JAZZ BAND**	JOHN BYE'S BAY CITY JAZZ BAND
DOWNBEAT ALL STAR JAZZ BAND		"WEE THREE" with PETER HOCKING DRUMS

FRIDAY, AUG. 28
MELBOURNE TOWN HALL

BOOK NOW AT MYERS, ALLANS, CLEMENS
6/6 TO 12/6

WHO'S WHO ... Tonight ...

John Bye's BAY CITY JAZZ BAND ... John Ellis (clar.), Iven Cocking (trom.), Alan Zavod (piano), Terry Villis (banjo), Ray Evans (drums), Ian Cocking (bass) and JOHN BYE (trumpet and leader), and tonight is a first for the boys.

Alex Hutchinson's "GROUP" ... John Fordham (drums), Joe McConechy (bass), Frank Gow (piano) and Alex Hutchinson (baritone/clar./alto). All the musicians have appeared in early Downbeat Jazz Concerts and today hold permanent positions in music here. Joe McConechy toured England recently with Frank Johnson.

NIGEL HUNT'S RAGTIME BAND ... Lee Treanor (banjo), Peter Clohesy (drums), Dick Barnes (bass), Roger Janes (trom.), Richard Miller (clar.) and NIGEL HUNT (TRUMPET AND LEADER). Nigel is from England and is married to Pat Purchase, the vocalist with the Yarra Yarra Jazz Band. Lee Treanor was banjoist with the same group for a few years.

HOT SANDS JAZZ BAND ... Graeme Bennett (leader and drummer), Frank Turville (trumpet), Campbell Burnap (trom.), Paul Martin (clar.), Willie Watt (banjo), Ken Sluce (bass). Ex Melbourne New Orleans Jazz Band members are now in this combination, making it about the strongest jazz around town.

RED ONION JAZZ BAND ... Ean Clyne has now joined the group on piano, adding another Old Scotch boy to the Band. W. & G. Records will be releasing their future recordings, which are big sellers on the local and interstate market.

MAX REED TRIO ... PAUL VEITH (bass), ALAN SMITH (drums) and MAX REED (piano). Alan will also be featured tonight in the 2nd Drum Battle. The group plays three nights each week at the Downbeat Jazz Club—Wednesday, Friday and Saturday —and is probably the most popular modern trio in Melbourne.

DRUM BATTLE ... again to end the concert ... more of a drumming exhibition than a battle. Tonight the three drummers featured are Kevin Murphy, Alan Smith and Allan Turnbull, courtesy of the PLAYBOY CLUB.

Margaret Roadknight, a Folk Singer, who is gaining popularity in quite a few Coffee Houses ... and this is her first Downbeat — and, in her own words, she bills herself as the World's Tallest Folk Singer.

Brendon Hanley's Melbourne Ballads should be as original as his Blowflies appearances. For folk who missed the Blowflies, they will be appearing shortly at the Downbeat Jazz Club ... at a special one-night stand.

Geoff Brooke, our Compere (a KZ man), has been in the top bracket of the Music Business since well pre war. A fine vocalist, he has appeared with every name band in Australia, makes regular TV guest spots on I.M.T., etc., and has been compering Downbeat for many years now ... and his easy going style makes him many friends from all age groups of the Downbeat audience.
Geoff's Supper Club session on 3KZ ... for the very latest in modern music ... has one of the best ratings in Radio.

THE DOWNBEAT AWARD GOES THIS MONTH TO THE YOUNG GENTLEMAN WHO SOLD DOWNBEAT JAZZ POSTERS FOR 1/- EACH AT A JAZZ DANCE LAST SATURDAY. Seeing you can obtain them free at Clemens, his profit margin was fairly high.

13 - HIGH SCHOOL BLUES

After the Downbeat incident, I was called up to the headmaster's office to face a different type of music. I would have preferred to be anywhere else but sitting outside the headmaster's office waiting for a committee to set my destiny. Also present was my maths teacher and my father, complete with his clerical collar. After a lecture from the headmaster on the importance of achieving a good education, the maths teacher made a statement, and I was asked to choose between playing in this so-called 'jazz band' or concentrating on my schoolwork. No compromise was on offer. All eyes were on me as I answered, 'No Contest'. The band was what defined me.

I was invited to change schools.

New School
At the same time that I was promoted to Sandringham Institute of Technology (Sandy Tech) a couple of other guys were also relocated to this all-boys, tough school. How tough? The joke was that the school had its own coroner.

One of the three guys relocating with me was known as 'Highett High's top fist'. The other kids at Sandy Tech didn't know which one it was, but that was short lived. Clearly, it was not me. I was the kid who played in a jazz band...and on TV, too. There's a rally call for the school bully!

Before long, the school's self-appointed enforcer hunted me out and roughed me up. He wanted to fight. I wanted to run. I got belted and I didn't like it.

I asked around about who was the toughest kid at Sandy Tech.

It was Harold. He wasn't particularly bright, but the offer of four shillings a week, secured me a big, strong minder. His first commission was to return the compliment to the coward who thumped me. No one bothered me again.

Sandringham Technical School wasn't a good fit with me. I had few like-minded friends there, and no interest in the trade classes on offer. I was hopeless at carpentry and totally out of place in the metalwork class. Technical drawing was okay but for the vicious, sadistic teacher who would wield the strap on our hands, both hands together at the same time, for the slightest misdemeanour. It's hard to hold a pencil with a red-raw hand. This fellow was also a very well known VFL field umpire, Flanagan by name. I should have asked Harold to have a chat with him, but I didn't.

As the warmer months arrived a few of us managed to get on to two sporting option lists, which wasn't noticed for many weeks. The swimming group thought we were on the cricket list, and vice versa.

We had Thursday afternoons off. Our leisure plan came to an abrupt end when the sporting masters compared notes and we were given gardening duties as punishment. The school's street frontage featured a bed of hydrangeas, which was to be weeded by us, albeit in the hot summer sun. I took exception to that. I borrowed four hacksaw blades from the metal workshop and some tape to make a handle. The unsupervised, reluctant weeding team used the improvised tools to 'trim' the hydrangea roots below the supporting soil bed. The team was moved on to other gardening duties the following week, but over the next few weeks it was compost for the school's floral street front display. I used the Sergeant Schultz defence, "I know nothing!"

The Postmaster General's Department (PMG) was recruiting telecommunication technicians in training and an officer visited the school in late 1964.

This was for me! I loved science, maths and electronics.

I took the enrolment test in November '64 and was selected for the January 1965 intake. Roll on the holiday break, heaps of holiday band jobs and goodbye Sandy Tech!

14 - MORE GIGS

The Bay City Jazz Band was working well and I had a training job set to commence in late January 1965. The band continued to appear on In Melbourne Tonight, and enjoyed quite a high profile, albeit to the displeasure of a few jazz purists.

Lakes Entrance
In late December 1964 I was offered a gig for the band over the Christmas holiday period in the resort town of Lakes Entrance. We were to play six nights a week over three weeks. Some of the guys couldn't get time off, so I had to make a few changes to the line-up.

This was a wonderful opportunity to earn 28 pounds per week each, and that was about equal to my father's weekly wage at the time.

The Mechanics Hall gig featured two bands, our traditional jazz band and a modern quintet. The young audience didn't like, or understand, the modern stuff too much. Russell Smith on trumpet and Lance Dixon on tenor sax were the saving grace for that band. Russell was a very hot, young trumpet player, who could play any style of jazz.

My band played all the old standards that the young audience knew and loved The problems started when the guys realised that we were all staying on site unless we individually made other accommodation arrangements. That was not really an option as the town was booked out months in advance.

The promoter, who happened to be the drummer in the other band, set up the back rooms at the venue with army surplus style, stretcher beds, and we shared the double shower and toilet block. The kitchen was ordinary, at best. It was pretty 'blokey'. Some of the guys made other questionable sleeping arrangements when presented with that option. I sure copped a fair few complaints from some of my band members but I reminded them that the money was very good and, as compensation, I had arranged to have our first week's pay in advance. Allan

Zavod told me he didn't think he would be able to last three weeks in these living conditions, but he would give it a try. Yes, it was pretty awful. Early into the second week Allan's parents turned up.

They were horrified with the living conditions and took him to their accommodation for a couple of nights He missed the interaction with the guys and was happy to return.

To my terror, a few days later my parents turned up in their little green Toyota Corolla. They may have had a call from Anne Zavod; who knows? But, here they were, unannounced. Fair enough, there was no phone at the hall. I told them that some of the boys were still asleep and we should go out for lunch. I asked the guys to clean up a bit, and get rid of any evidence of booze. Allan and I were teetotallers in those days, but the other guys were not. After lunch I gave my folk a quick tour of the venue, explained that everything was in order, and after all I was nearly seventeen. Phew! Off they tootled.

Towards the end of the third week there was an increase in the tension between some of the guys. John Ellis was tired of playing the same old trad standards and would have much preferred to be playing with Russell, who was a far better trumpet player than I. I knew that, but John also knew who the paymaster was. Between the two bands we had up to 12 guys living together in the back rooms of a crappy hall in Lakes Entrance.

Overall, it was an amazing experience, but never again, thanks.

We sure were ready for the re-opening of our regular Saturday night at 431. The crowds of teenage dancers turned up, paid their 6/6d, then on with the show.

We had a series of guest artists including the marvellously entertaining, Yogi Bear (aka John Cawthan). John was the banjo player/vocalist with the Derek Harris' Driftwood Jazz Band. Derek was my trumpet teacher and mentor at the time. Yogi Bear (let's call him by that handle) would come on stage at 9 pm. He liked the big entrance, so he'd give me the nod, we'd play a vamp intro, and he would appear from the back of the hall through the crowded dance floor. The audience loved it. I was always aware that we had to entertain our audience, not play at them.

As Ray Evans had a driver's licence and I still had a year to go before I was old enough to apply, we decided to buy a car together. It was always difficult getting to and from gigs and I was forever asking the other guys for a lift. Ray found a Wolseley 6/80 saloon for about 600 pounds that really appealed. The U.K. police used such fine vehicles in the 1950s. Ours didn't have a bell on the front, but it was black and had suicide opening back doors. One of the back doors didn't always want to co-operate and the starter motor was dodgy. Whenever anything went wrong Ray would leave the car at my place and I'd try to fix the old girl. The clutch cable gave way one night on the way home from Heidelberg West and we had to nurse the old Wolseley home in second gear, without stopping.

Ray was often mistaken for a prominent St Kilda footballer, Carl Ditterich, and he used this to his advantage. Ray always seemed to attract the most gorgeous girls but it was always short lived. Ray used everyone and everything to his advantage. He knew it's not what you know, it's how you use who you know.

Meanwhile, I quite enjoyed my day job at the PMG (Tooronga) Technicians School. I had a number of really terrific instructors including Ian Richardson with whom I recently reconnected at the Victorian Jazz Club. He approached me and asked, "Didn't you used to be trainee John Bye?" He remembered me getting him tickets to be in the audience at In Melbourne Tonight. What are the odds of this happening?

That was over half a century ago.

I earned my first (official) pay packet at the PMG training school. We were paid fortnightly in cash. It was a work place/school hybrid that I could manage, given my band commitments. Pop star, Normie Rowe, was in the year above me, but the second year trainees didn't mix with the first year guys. That wasn't cool.

New Directions

As the year rolled on there were more rumblings in the band about our repertoire and line-up. The audiences were becoming more aware of the current airplay material. We needed to change direction.

Firstly we dropped the prefix 'jazz' from the name.

John Ellis would play sax instead of clarinet, Terry Villis on guitar...banjo go away. No trombone required. Sorry Ivan. Peter Wilson (bass) was replaced by a very young Joe Gorski on bass guitar. Allan Zavod, by far our best player, acquired a Farfisa electronic keyboard. Incidentally, I can't remember where I found bass player, Joe Gorski. He was a very young, inexperienced player, but a pretty good player and he looked the part. I still see his family name on massive trucks and earthmoving equipment all around Australia.

In 1966 The Bay City Band appeared on IMT with the new line-up and we were booked for a number of casual gigs as well as our 431 regular Saturday nights. Bob Phillips (GTV9) was managing the band at this stage and he arranged a recording session at Channel Nine. We made our first (and only) single record, on the Vamp label. The 'A' side featured a tune written by Tony Barber, 'Blue Day'.

Tony was the rhythm guitarist with the hugely successful rock band, Billy Thorpe and The Aztecs. Our little seven-inch, single record charted at number 40 on the 3DB Top Forty in March 1966, just behind 'The Fortune Teller' by The Throb.

The top selling forty singles lists were compiled from sales at a handful of record outlets. I was aware that Coles Store 200 was in this unique group.

I arranged for as many people I could muster to purchase a copy there. I also arranged to buy back our record, and resell them at gigs. Airplay was crucial to climbing up the charts. We achieved very little airplay, but we did scream up to #28 in one survey for one week of the three in the charts.

Still, there were rumblings of discontent in the band.

The direction the band was heading was probably right for the times, but the line-up was not.

I contracted a dose of tonsillitis and ended up in Sandringham Hospital.

I was advised that I needed a few weeks rest without playing. (A rest also for my audience.) John Ellis suggested that Russell Smith should replace me (which is what he had dreamed of since Lakes Entrance) and other line-up changes be made, permanently. Neither John Ellis nor Ray Evans discussed any of their plans with me. I actually thought it was a good move at the time, but the way it was done was pretty poor form.

They replaced Joe (bass guitar) and Terry (lead guitar) with much more experienced rock players.

Allan Zavod later told me he wanted no part in this plan. He was very uncomfortable with John Ellis' coup.

It didn't work out well for Ray in the following months either.

My hijacked band was to be called 'The Bay City Set'.

The conspirators approached 431 and completed the coup.

I was not happy with the way this panned out.

I had registered the business name of my band, 'Bay City', on July 6th, 1966. John Ellis and Ray Evans stole that name and I wasn't going to let that pass.

I had a 'cease and desist' letter sent to the relevant parties and the Bay City Set was much like the Monty Python parrot. Totally bereft of life. John Ellis and Russell Smith rehashed the embers, dumped Ray Evans and came up with The Ram Jam Big Band. Russell Smith was a great player and I went on to work with him years later on both my albums for Vince Jones.

Ray Evans was involved with Go-Set pop magazine and established a talent booking and management agency with Michael Gudinski (Evans-Gudinski). They later fell out...big time. Ray went on to 'manage' a number of big names in the entertainment industry, with some interesting results.

Read 'Difficult Woman' by Renee Geyer. (Published 2000 by Harper Collins)

It appears that Ray may have left a trail of destruction.

The Bay City Band

HITMAKERS
By CHRISTOPHER DE KRETSER

The change from jazz

JAZZ dances which were once the rage in Melbourne have been gradually dying.

Up until the end of last year they gained one of their few remaining props from "431" in St. Kilda.

But this dance went mod in the middle of January.

The change not only affected the dance but also the Bay City Jazz Band who had been playing there for the past 18 months.

They soon became the Bay City Band, as they changed their style to play rhythm and blues.

"All of us except our drummer Ray Evans had to change our instruments," said John Bye, 18, the leader of the group.

"We swapped the trumpet, clarinet, piano, banjo and bass for a harmonica, sax, organ, and guitars," he said.

"The change has been quite successful and the crowds at '431' have become bigger and more enthusiastic.

"And we are improving our playing every week as we learn new numbers and get accustomed to this change of style," he said.

The other members of the band are John Ellis, 19; Allan Zavod, 18; Terry Villio, 19; Joe Gorski, 16, and Ray Evans, 19.

The group began playing together about two years ago.

About 18 months ago they got their big break when they were offered the job at "431."

They have been playing there regularly on Saturday nights since.

However, in the next few months the band could become even more successful.

They have made a record which has just been released.

One side, called "Agent 098," is an original composition of John Ellis and John Bye.

The other side is a tune composed by Tony Barber, a former member of the Aztecs, called "Blueday."

3DB TOP 40

This Week	Last Week		Weeks In
1	1	THESE BOOTS ARE MADE FOR WALKING (Nancy Sinatra)	7
2	12	SECOND HAND ROSE (Barbara Streisand)	3
3	2	MICHELLE (Overlanders) (David and Jonathan)	5
4	4	THE CARNIVAL IS OVER (The Seekers)	21
5	11	BREAKING POINT (Normie Rowe)	2
6	3	AS TEARS GO BY (The Rolling Stones)	7
7	6	GLORIA (Them)	12
8	5	THE FORTUNE TELLER (The Throb)	5
9	9	SOMEDAY ONEDAY (The Seekers)	5
10	7	WALKIN' IN THE SAND (M.P.D. Ltd.)	7
11	10	TENNESSEE WALTZ SONG (Ray Brown)	10
12	8	SOMEDAY (Tony Barber)	7
13	13	LISTEN PEOPLE (Herman's Hermits)	7
14		NOWHERE MAN (The Beatles)	1
15	20	THE ANGELS LISTENED IN (The Cherokees)	3
16	23	I FOUGHT THE LAW (The Bobby Fuller Four)	2
17	15	MY LOVE (Petula Clark)	8
18	18	LIGHTNIN' STRIKES (Lou Christy)	6
19	16	THE BEST IN AFRICA (The Group)	6
20	25	IF SHE FINDS OUT (The Twilights)	3
21	14	THE CHEATER (Bob Kuman and The In Men)	8
22	21	CRYSTAL CHANDELIER (Vic Dana)	12
23	19	YOU'VE GOT WHAT IT TAKES (Merv Benton)	8
24		HITCH HIKER (Bobby and Laurie)	1
25	29	DON'T TAKE ME OVER (The Swingin' Blue Jeans)	3
26	32	UNTIL IT'S TIME FOR YOU TO GO (Buffy Sainte Marie)	2
27	27	TELL HIM I'M NOT HOME (Normie Rowe)	18
28	17	GIRLS, GIRLS, GIRLS (The Fourmost)	8
29	22	BARBARA ANN (The Beach Boys)	9
30	31	MY GENERATION (The Who)	10
31		BEFORE YOUR TIME (Mark Wynter)	1
32	24	LOVE LETTERS (Billy Thorpe)	13
33		GIRL (The Truth)	1
34	38	WOMAN (Peter and Gordon)	2
35	34	WOMEN (The Easybeats)	9
36	36	QUE SERA SERA (Normie Rowe)	28
37	39	INSIDE LOOKING OUT (The Animals)	2
38	26	BLUE DAY (Bay City Band)	4
39		THE ONE ON THE LEFT (Johnny Cash)	1
40	40	JENNY TAKE A RIDE (Mitch Ryder)	4

The Sun, Friday, April 1, 1966

15 - UBANGI JAZZ BAND

In August 1966 Bob Phillips asked me to put together a band for a special 'New Faces' edition for In Melbourne Tonight. It was a last-minute inclusion to balance the program content. We were to play 'The Isle Of Capri'. I had a week or so to get this together. I rang around and managed to cobble a workable line-up. It was difficult finding a good, young trombone player for this one-off gig. One of the guys suggested Steve Waddell, a very fine player, if a little prickly. He was good, and he knew it. When I phoned Steve, he made it clear that he wasn't interested in playing that tune, especially in my scratch band. I mentioned in passing that the one-tune-gig paid $16 each.

He played well.

At this time our family was living in Royal Avenue, Sandringham, not far from the famed union leader, and later Australian Prime Minister, Bob Hawke. (I know how to drop names.) Soon after, we moved to Auburn and Bob didn't even notice.

The Ubangi Jazz Band

I decided to tidy up the lineup from this IMT special and form another band, and what resulted became The Ubangi Jazz Band. I'd met so many really keen, young players and I just needed to stabilise the mix. I didn't have a drummer in mind, so I advertised in the classified pages of the Age (ICPOTA). Richard Opat 'auditioned' for the part. Not only did I find a fabulous drummer, I found my best friend...to this very day. (No one else applied for either role.) The line-up had a few changes over the next couple of years, but the Ubangi band was fun, and many enduring friendships were established and remain to this day.

Looking back, I see the The Ubangi Jazz Band was only ever to be antidote to the toxic end to my previous, much loved, Bay City Jazz Band. I wanted to play some trad jazz with guys who had no agenda and just wanted to have some fun. I knew my strengths and weaknesses. I also had a plan to travel around Australia with my new girlfriend. Ubangi; Ubetcha!

One of our more memorable gigs, for all the wrong reasons, was at the Tatra Inn at Mt Buffalo, in snowfields off-season. I plastered posters up around Wangaratta and I'd used a PA system, with huge horn speakers mounted on my Austin A55, to announce the forthcoming gig. Nothing worked and our adoring audience were nowhere to be found.

However, one of the 'single' guys in the band made friends with an under-worked barmaid. They seemed to get on very well together over the long weekend. (Technically, we were all single.)

The Ubangi band played some terrific gigs and a couple of absolutely horrid ones. I remember setting up for a twenty-first birthday party at a bowling club in the Eastern suburbs of Melbourne. As the first guests arrived, someone called out, "Oh no, not a jazz band! I hate jazz."

This was just the beginning of a tough evening. We struggled through the first set, and then the hosts set up trestle tables down the centre of the hall.

The local Chinese restaurant provided saucepans full of their signature dishes (including #42 chicken and cashews) and it was self-service for all.

Paper plates and plastic cutlery at ten paces.

Some hungry punters tended to overfill their flimsy plates and the floor copped a hiding.

Still, there was plenty of beer on tap, so the show went on.

After the floor was cleaned and cleared of trestle tables, we continued our performance.

Out in the back room, behind the stage, was a large, unlocked trophy cabinet. I grabbed three or four of the bigger, more ornate pieces, and offered them up as temporary prizes for the best dancers. Our clarinet player, Peter (Magic) Mason, a very skilled magician, added his contribution to the evening's entertainment, and we had the audience totally on side.

Magic Mason is very active on the Melbourne jazz scene and a much valued friend as I write.

This band had a wonderful camaraderie. Egos were never out of order, and it was just darn good fun.

Ubangi Jazz Band
One of the best bands in the country ...
in the city; maybe not!

Left to right:
Russel Munger, Richard Opat, Len Watterson,
John Bye, Peter Bennett, Mike Cousins

Peter Mason later joined the band on clarinet,
sadly we can't find any pics.

16 - AUBURN

In late 1966 my father was posted to Auburn Methodist church and we moved into the manse, next door to the magnificent, heritage listed church. The buildings are still remarkably intact given that they date back to the late 1880s. My sisters had all moved on and so it was just my parents and myself, in this stately, two-storey mansion.

As a Methodist Ladies College student, my mother had lived in this very house, when her father was the minister there some 50 years earlier. In the backyard the stables, where her father had his horse and carts housed, the buildings are still in use. I parked my car there in the late 60s as I didn't have a horse or a cart.

In 1968 I joined ATV Channel 0 as a trainee cameraman and worked on a few pop music shows plus the usual talking heads programs. As the lowest paid cameraman, I was rostered on to the Saturday late night shift with Deadly Ernest (floor manager, Ralph Baker) introducing horror movies. This attracted a huge cult following.

I took a keen interest in television production techniques and was also a filmmaker in training at the time.

As it happened, my sister Margie, Alan and family moved in to 81 Oxley Rd, Auburn, whilst their home was being renovated. So, our household swelled to seven, with Margie, Alan, Cathy (4) and Heathie (1). I loved the extra company and all the distractions that brought.

The band days came to an end, for now.

My girlfriend, Helen Davenport, and I shared an interest in travelling around this mighty continent, amongst other things. However, I'm sure we also shared one major underlining aim to be free of parental controls.

Helen's father had been a major in the army and his life revolved around the goings on at the RSL. His mates were all returned servicemen.

I had a strong feeling that I would not have been his preferred son-in law. A teetotaller, son of a minister and absolutely opposed to the Vietnam conflict that Australia was being dragged into. I was an out-and-out conscientious objector.

I ticked all the wrong boxes for Major Davenport: but I must add that 'Buster Davenport', as his many friends knew him, was a real genuine 'fair dinkum' bloke. He was loud, proud and a heap of fun.

My father and I attended a number of anti-Vietnam war rallies, but not together.

All twenty-year-old males were required to register for the National Service lottery. In 1968 I was in the draw, which was based on the date of birth. When the card arrived in the mail to advise me the result, my father called me into his front room office. He explained that we needed a plan should I be called up. The fact that Helen and I were engaged added an extra dimension.

He opened the official envelope that would announce the result of the draw. This was the only time I ever witnessed my father shed a tear. My National Service call up was deferred. What a relief.

In those monochrome times, most young people coupled up, engaged, married and settled down. My sisters all married young, and here was I well and truly in the queue.

Prior to Helen and I commencing our travels, one little detail had to be attended to. Today, you'd just head off with your partner, but in the late sixties, we were expected to be married.

Ridiculous! but that's simply how it was.

The plan was to marry in late March 1969 and get some space between the lifestyle we were expected to live and what we actually wanted. I bought a second-hand, 14' 9" Franklin caravan. It had a very basic layout including two single beds, a little table and a tiny kitchenette.

My carpenter brother-in-law, Robert, and I, stripped the van, and he rebuilt the interior, to our (Helen's) specifications. It was transformed into an amazingly comfortable, micro home on wheels.

The twenty-ninth of March went almost perfectly to plan. We were married by my father (how many people can say that?) at Auburn Methodist Church with the reception being held at 8 St Georges Road, Elsternwick.

Another brother-in-law was the official photographer, however, owing to camera problems, no photos of the reception exist. It's a pity that a few guests didn't have smart phones, but they hadn't been invented.

Here's the thing I didn't know, until years later.

As our reception was an alcohol free event, my new father-in-law had arranged an after party for his group of army friends. Major Davenport was a real, larger than life character who liked to blow the head off a frothy beer, or three. It would have been a real hoot.

MLC girls: Kathleen (my mother) and Florence Scholes

Lillian, Kathleen and Florence with their father circa 1923

17 - HEADING WEST

Leaving Melbourne

Helen and I planned to travel around Australia in our little caravan for a year or so. When we headed off a few friends and relatives gathered to say farewell and ensure that we actually left. We had the predictable cries of 'see you in a week or two'.

After arriving in Adelaide via Robe, we needed to work to top up the travel funds. Helen worked at a childcare centre and I took a job as a forklift driver at a door factory. I had no idea that these machines have rear wheel steering. I was less than hopeless at loading anything, let alone four palettes each holding twenty-five doors, at a time. This was a union factory, and I was told to stop work immediately the horn sounded and take the seven-minute smoko break.

I had a full load on the fork when the horn sounded. So, I stopped.

While I was having the tea break as demanded, the forklift unloaded itself, crashing down with few surviving doors.

I was offered other, simpler duties and encouraged not to go anywhere near the loading bay.

I had no intention of staying any longer than absolutely necessary.

At this time we were waiting for word that the Eyre Highway, across the Nullarbor Plain had re-opened after heavy rains. The road trip between Adelaide and Kalgoorlie was just shy of 2,200 km with about 600km of rough, un-made surface. It was almost impossible for two-wheel drive vehicles, especially towing a caravan, to get through at times. After our six-week stopover in Adelaide, the road was declared safe and we set off.

It took us a few days to reach the West Australian gold mining town of Kalgoorlie. This was a taste of the Wild West. It was a very blokey town, rough and ready, and infamous for its rows of street-front brothels.

Our stay in the twin towns of Kalgoorlie-Boulder was longer than planned as

Helen had picked up some horrid bug along the way and ended up in the local hospital. Boy, that was a real eye-opener in the late sixties and she couldn't get out quick enough.

We were now running on empty in the travel funds department. We soon became aware that there were plenty of jobs in the new nickel-mining town of Kambalda, some sixty km south-east. Western Mining Corporation (WMC) ran and owned the town of Kambalda. We both landed well-paid work and stayed about nine months in Kambalda. I was working as an instrument technician, thanks to my PMG training, and Helen set up the new kindergarten. My work included installing telephones in the underground crib (lunch) rooms, hundreds of feet below ground. At the Silver Lake mine shaft this involved being taken underground in a kibble, a bucket big enough for four or five men. This was round and the shaft was square. Getting in and out was quite dangerous. If I had to get off at the 300-ft level, there were still five hundred feet of sheer drop to the shaft's lowest level. It was quite terrifying getting in and out of this giant bucket.

After a fatality on site, the kibble was replaced with a secure cage. Once the men were at their required level below ground, typically, 300 feet, 400 feet up to the 800-ft level, the cage was replaced with an ore skip that would run for an eight-hour shift, taking nickel ore to the surface. It was dirty, noisy and dusty work... but well paid.

My work underground usually took an hour or so to complete, and then I had seven hours to kill before returning to the surface. I had a hard hat lamp and a little pick in my toolbox, so I could rummage around to try to find a little speck of gold. Alas, I only ever found 'iron pyrite' aka fools gold. Thankfully, I only went underground at the Silver Lake mine about eight or ten times. At the 'Durkin' incline shaft, we walked in and out. It was just amazing to see what went on underground. The massive machines are all low profile to fit into the confined spaces, but there was some very serious heavy engineering happening way below the surface. The machine operators at the ore face earn huge money and deserve every cent.

The company paid for us to return to Melbourne so that Helen could procure the necessary equipment to set up the kindergarten. This was an extraordinary life-changing experience for me, but I didn't know that at the time.

The two main kindergarten supply shops in Melbourne treated their customers as an inconvenient disruption. I remember (again) thinking, 'there's a business opportunity if ever I saw one'. I'll come back to that thought.

It was an interesting time; living in the married quarters caravan park, and taking weekend trips out into the Goldfields' ghost towns, the likes of Broad Arrow and Ora Banda. We experienced the most amazing electrical storms with lightning amplified by the metallic ore rich landscapes. Quite often the most threatening sky shows came from the dry storms. No place for the faint hearted.

WMC discovered massive nickel reserves underneath the township settlement. They decided to move the town 4 km west. Well-established houses, the school and the little shopping centre all were moved.

Everything changed when the unions moved in, and the casual work descriptions were thrown out. I didn't have the formal qualifications to do the job I had, although I did have my WA restricted electrical licence. I was forced to join the Electrical Trades Union and from time to time they would hold a 'stop work meeting' for no apparent reason other than to flex their power. The unions did tidy up a wide range of safety issues that the company had neglected.

Kambalda Nickel Operations (KNO) was not a particularly safe workplace when I started there in 1969. We often heard about on-site fatalities.

It was time to move on. We travelled south to the coastal town of Esperance. No work was on offer there, but I displayed a 'Radio Repairs' sign in the caravan park, and picked up a few clients. Then we headed northwest to Manjimup, where we picked apples for about six weeks. A Seventh-day Adventist family owned the orchard; consequently we were not permitted to work on Saturdays. Our host would saddle up a couple of horses for us, and we'd go bush for the day, very slowly. I was not built for horse riding and the sweaty beasts made me sneeze.

Perth

Early in 1970 we arrived in Perth.

Beautiful white sand and surf beaches greeted us. What a contrast to settings of the past year, with the exception of the rugged Esperance coastline. We set up our home at the Sorrento caravan park and were back in the workforce within weeks. This is when I joined the ABC as a television cameraman. I use the word 'joined' as it was a production team, and I loved my time there. My official job description was technical operator. We were trained in camera, audio, lighting and vision mixing. I was stationed in studio 61. Six indicated WA (by postcode) and one was the number of TV studios we had in Perth. The crew were pretty fixed in their area of expertise and cameraman was my preferred role. We did have a very impressive OB (outside broadcast) van and I also loved the football and cricket gigs. The ABC was a great training ground and I took advantage of any tutorials and training courses on offer, but the ABC paid poorly. I loved the studio atmosphere and the 1:30 pm to 9:30 pm usual shift times but I was not content with the super thin pay packet after having big dollars in Kambalda. I had my own 16mm movie camera and I moonlighted on a few film projects and even made a little training film for my previous employer, WMC.

In the early 1970s the mining boom in WA was in full flight. Helen and I connected with a fast-talking American couple (and their slow-talking little daughter) who wanted to travel to the goldfields and document the mining boom on film. Kent Wade described himself as a photographer; he had the financial backing and I had the technical knowhow, plus Helen and I had first-hand experience living in the goldfields of Western Australia. I resigned from the ABC and we hooked up our new 25' Viscount caravan to our brand new Toyota FJ40 short wheelbase Land Cruiser. Our American associates had a similar, sponsored rig. He had a way of getting 'freebies'.

The plan was to make a 90-minute documentary contrasting the past gold rush days to the current nickel mining boom. We planned to then take our movie and still pics exhibition on the road, literally. We would do the town hall circuit that the likes of the Leyland Brothers and Malcolm Douglas had made so popular.

We would also document this tour around Australia on film. It was a very ambitious project in so many aspects, not the least being that we hardly knew the Wade family.

Our first Goldfields stopover was the almost 'ghost town' of Coolgardie. We discovered some really interesting characters here and we really were off to a flying start. Locals told us about an old hermit miner who lived in a shack halfway along the water pipeline between Coolgardie and Kalgoorlie. He had access to water but no other creature comforts that we need to survive. He happily demonstrated his primitive 'dry blowing' gold-panning device and loved performing to camera. He told us about another old timer who kept goats, two hundred of them, way out in this remote, harsh country wilderness. We continued on to Kalgoorlie and I was able to negotiate a seat on a flying doctor rescue flight to the edge of the great Australian desert. The footage was priceless, as was the whole experience. The documentary concluded with an interview with Ken Shirley, the man who pegged the Poseidon claim. During the Poseidon Bubble the share price went from $0.80 to $280. Bugger! If only we knew then...

Someone once said to Ken " I hear you've found nickel son, pity it wasn't gold!"

On the strength of that, we titled our film Pity It Wasn't Gold. We returned to Perth where I edited the footage while Kent processed and mounted his stills. The editing process was time consuming and a huge learning curve for me. I had to hire a 16mm editing suite and worked late into the night for some three weeks or so. Kent arranged the World Premiere at Subiaco town hall and then on to Fremantle town hall.

We had next to no real publicity and the screening bombed out. Kent soon lost all interest in proceeding any further at that stage. We were all feeling rather deflated, but we had a pretty good documentary to market. We set up a meeting at Kent's flat to formulate a plan. He said that he needed a couple of weeks to meet with his sponsors and prepare a marketing program. We needed a break too. Helen and I turned up at the Wades on the prescribed date. Their flat was empty; they were gone and we never saw them or the one and only print of 'Pity It Wasn't Gold' again.

The novelty of living in a caravan and using caravan park facilities was wearing thin, even though we had upgraded to a twenty-five foot Viscount, with an on-board shower.

We moved to a little flat in Maylands and couldn't believe just how much space this afforded us. This is living!

By now, we were both working at jobs that were purely stop-gap, unfulfilling, and somewhat moribund.

Goodbye Perth

After three years away, we decided to drive home to Melbourne, over the top of Australia via Darwin.

We missed the family and the 'olds' were getting, well, older. I understand that now; and that's my plan, too.

For the major drive home I chose the most unsuitable vehicle possible. A Toyota, Ford or a Holden?

No. I bought a third-hand, Renault R16, front-wheel drive, family hatch, suitable only for touring between wineries in the south of France. I doubt if anyone north of Quinns Rocks had ever seen such a vehicle. I must add that it did have comfy, leather seats. The fuel cap was well secured behind the rear number plate. I loved watching the bowser boys trying to find how to refuel the thing.

(Remember bowser boys? I was one, once.)

As the boot was hopelessly deficient, I fitted the car with a purpose built roof rack. Oh yes, we also had a two-person canoe to join us on the 7,500 km trip home. This may sound ridiculous, but with the canoe mounted on top of the R16, we also had extra storage space. To Helen's great credit, she went along with yet another harebrained adventure. It also probably tells you, dear reader, something about the writer.

Kalbarri, at the mouth of the Murchison River, was our first camping stopover. This is where I started to film our return trip on my much loved Beaulieu 16mm movie film camera. Kalbarri Gorge is absolutely stunning as are the coastal blowholes. Incidentally, these blowholes were intentionally modified (blown up) by the military during the Second World War as they could be used as a landmark for enemy ships. Fancy blowing up blowholes!

Anyway, they can still perform a twenty-metre spurt on a rough day. (Don't try that at home!)

We were off to a great start.

We had a little tent and folding camp stretchers, the most uncomfortable I could find, as it turned out. Our washing machine was a bucket with a lid, riding in the canoe. The rough road surface performed the agitating and with a couple of changes of water, the washing was done.

Sleeping in the car was most uncomfortable, but in some circumstances, the safest option. Driving after dusk was dangerous due to the abundant wildlife, and the need to find a suitable campsite. One night particularly comes to mind. We were heading towards Broome and just couldn't find a suitable campsite.

Eventually we pulled over into a secluded truck lay-by. We couldn't drive any further that night. We slept in the car, but around midnight, a Ford F100 pickup pulled into the lay-by. A guy got out, emptied all sorts of stuff, including ropes, camping gear and fishing rods, from the back, and he and his passenger climbed in.

We were very uneasy about our uninvited neighbours, but we had to tough it out. Morning came after a long night, and it became clear that we had nothing to worry about. The young guy said that his girlfriend was shit scared until she spotted our car. They had seen us tottering along days ago, and thought we looked pretty safe.

After Broome came Fitzroy Crossing. Oh, joy! A beautiful free camping site on the Fitzroy River welcomed us. There were a number of young travellers setting up camp here in these magnificent grounds, a few of whom we had met along the way. This was a perfect stopping off point to recharge the batteries.

At last we had the perfect launching place for our canoe. We'd schlepped it all this way and only used it twice since leaving Perth.

The camping ground was right at the entrance of Geikie Gorge.

Is there a more stunning national park? The river is home to the fresh-water Johnson River crocodile.

These are the narrow snout crocs that mainly eat fish, not humans. They may take a snap at the unwelcome intruder, but it would only be a love bite.

On launching our canoe, we were warned that the odd rogue salt-water crock had been sighted in the Fitzroy River from time to time. That's also a good reason to camp well away from the water's edge.

As we paddled our canoe up the 30-metre deep gorge into the remains of the ancient limestone reef, we saw many small sunbathing crocks slide down the banks into the river. They ranged from one to two and a half metres in length and soon motivated us to turn around and head back to camp. We were only separated from the croc-infested water by a flimsy, thin layer of fibreglass. We did venture out a couple more times but not so far on those occasions.

We visited another fresh-water gorge on the way to Katherine. Again, we launched the canoe but as we were the only people there, it didn't feel safe paddling around in uncharted waters.

Travelling there on rough, unmade tracks, the Renault took a beating. It was far too low for this loose, rocky, surface. The fuel line was smashed before we made it back to the main road, and the R16 stopped, dead.

We'd had previous, minor fuel line problems before reaching Broome, and I had bought a length of plastic tube for running repairs. I had to re-route the fuel supply to enable us to limp into the nearest petrol station, 170 km up the road. Helen needed to nurse the spare petrol jerry can between her knees, with the flexible temporary fuel line in place.

The guys at the petrol station had never seen a Renault R16. I can understand why they treated us like complete fools, bringing such a car in for repairs. We had to stay overnight before the car was ready to head off again.

Katherine Gorge was our next campsite. At the time, the ugly side of commercialism hadn't crept into any of these spectacular natural waterways. Again the canoe enabled us to explore the area and we came across a marvellous little crystal clear pool and waterfall. We hauled the canoe up onto the bank, had a swim and took a shower. To our horror, we spotted a motorboat, with 6 or 8 people on board, heading our way. Our clothes were in the canoe on the other side of the river. We didn't even have a towel. We hid in the jungle until they were out of sight. Nowadays, you wouldn't even bat an eyelid. We were such prudes, although I think I had a touch of the 'Tarzan' spirit about me.

Darwin

The much punished R16 was not happy. I had a mechanic check it over in Darwin and he suggested it was far too overloaded to make it back to Melbourne. It was going to cost big dollars to prepare Renault for the return trip down the east coast. The canoe had to go, for a start.

I made some handwritten signs saying,

'CANOE FOR SALE $300 Apply Within'. (Free Delivery within Darwin area)

I parked in the main street, near the town hall, and sat in the canoe, which was on the R16 roof rack.

I drew quite a few weird looks, and a few tourists scrambled for their Kodak Instamatics, to get some pics but within 90 minutes I had a punter.

After a four-day week, well it seemed like a week, in this hot, sticky, humid region, we headed down the Stuart Highway to Mataranka, adding a few days in Kakadu National Park. Mataranka thermal pools were high on our 'must visit' list. We stumbled on a major Indigenous festival that attracted a BBC TV crew, which was following the famous British character actor, Derek Nimmo. He had a British upper crust persona and wasn't at all approachable. His claim to fame was that he had a cameo appearance in the Beatles movie, 'A Hard Day's Night'.

We spent a week in this magnificent national park, made famous by the 1902 book We of the Never Never.

As travel funds and allocated time were running short, the next stopover destination was Townsville, on the Queensland coast. The east coast was so much more commercial and suburban than we had experienced over the past few months.

We did stay in some beautiful seaside settings on the trip down, but Melbourne was calling. We stopped over in Sydney for a few days and Helen's parents came up to welcome us home. Buster took me to an RSL leagues club and showed me how to lose a dollar on the one armed bandits!

This 14'9" Franklin caravan was our home for about 18 months

Harnessing the winds on the Kambalda salt flats.

New prospects for old prospectors!
Coolgardie's famous Bailey Mine .. Today!

The Goat Lady of Bulong caring for her family of 200. "If I say Buttons, up will pop Buttons! Brendalee .... !

"Like all gold towns, they all go down."

The Royal Flying Doctor servicing the ½ million sq. miles of the Eastern Goldfields.

"For the major drive home I chose the most unsuitable vehicle possible. A Toyota, Ford or a Holden? No. I bought a third-hand, Renault R16".

When the car broke down, as it liked to, we'd boil the billy and survey the damage. This time it was just a matter of re-packing the wheel bearings with grease and limping into the next town.

18 - BACK HOME

Catching up with family and friends after more than three years away was pretty darn good, although some folk hadn't really noticed our absence, or didn't care for any details. Or both. That could damage one's ego…but it didn't.

I needed to get a fairly well paid job to position us for the young family program that was expected of such couples. We'd done the 'gap year' routine over the past three years or so. Helen went back to teaching.

After a short stint working for the giant electronic company Philips, I landed a sales position at Nidac, a security equipment manufacturer in Burwood. The chain smoking, electronics engineer who owned this company, David Nichols, was quite brilliant. David's 2 IC was Bruce Clift, equally brilliant, but with a different skill set. This little company had so much potential, and is still in business as I write.

I was on the road, which meant that I had my first ever, company car. We sold security equipment components to burglar alarm companies and to a number of resellers; the best known of these that I remember to this day was Dick Smith Electronics. He had a car radio business in Sydney and opened up a chain of electronic component stores. His office was above the bigger car radio store in Parramatta, Sydney. In these times, car radios were an optional, third party, extra. The entrance to his office was via an outside metal stairway, much like a fire escape.

My only meeting with Mr Smith was after he contacted us to discuss the purchase of the Nidac industry standard, 12V regulated power supply. David and Bruce coached me in all the finer technical details, and off to Sydney I went.

Dick sat at a big, older style desk. Behind him was a matrix of light globes. As I started my well-rehearsed sales pitch, the globes lit up, shouting 'NO'.

I was stopped in full flight by Mr Smith roaring with laughter. He was a real character.

Finally, 'YES', the globes finally spelt out, and I made a sale. My adrenalin level went up to eleven (on the audio scale).

While I was working at Nidac and researching kindergarten equipment suppliers, I worked on a few security alarm installations to keep my technical skills up to date and, of course, as a nice little earner. Helen and I were living in a very compact flat, above a marvellously stately home, in East Camberwell.

One evening I was working with a mate from Nidac, installing a video security system in a city pharmacy, when an ambulance went screaming up the top end of town. I mentioned to my associate that that was where my father was addressing a conference.

We completed the job late in the evening and when I returned home, my brother-in-law, Rob, was waiting for me in the driveway. He didn't have to say anything; I just knew.

It's still hard for me to recall this night.

My father was gone as was my mother's will to live.

Mum aged ten years over the next few weeks. She was not coping. Heather took a huge beating mentally, and all credit to her husband, Rob, who held things together for their family.

Meanwhile my youngest sister's marriage was finished and she too was overcome with grief. She had two young daughters, Alison and Yvonne. Their father had been an abusive, difficult fellow who wanted nothing to do with his little family, or his extended family for that matter. Mum was now living alone in the family home at 14 Central Road, Blackburn. Helen and I decided to move in.

She needed us and we were in a position to be there for her.

At this time, Roie was not coping at all well. Her world was collapsing around her so she, and her two little girls moved in too.

The population of 'Toad Hall' (as mum called it) swelled to six.

We had a full house and mum had a new lease on life.

This arrangement could only have ever been temporary, but it worked with everyone making concessions.

Roie's daughters now have families of their own on different sides of Australia and I sometimes wonder what memories they have of those times.

Is it healthy to repress difficult memories? I'm not sure.

I've done just that in the past, but has it been helpful? I think not.

Life settled down in Blackburn and it was time for us to move on. We bought a lovely little weatherboard home in an almost rural setting in Melbourne's outer eastern suburb of Mooroolbark.

Helen was back in the kindergarten teaching area, and from time to time needed to buy equipment. As I've mentioned earlier, for those who weren't paying attention, Melbourne had two main suppliers in this field, Kindergarten Supplies P/L & A R Whitelaw and Co. I found these retailers to be totally wanting in the manner they treated their bulk-buying customers. They were running glorified toyshops, and they deemed their cashed up clients to be an inconvenient disruption.

This industry needed a shakeup and I was up for it.

I thoroughly enjoyed my time at Nidac. The culture there was uplifting. David Nicholls was a charismatic leader, and on a few occasions he let me drive his huge, amazing, gas-guzzling, V8 Pontiac. I felt so super cool in this massive Yank tank. But I wasn't!

I did want to take on the challenge of establishing my own business. The thought of working for myself was overpowering, even from the days of selling Footy Records as a primary school kid.

I'd found another industry that really interested me and clearly offered me this opportunity.

I had to move on.

19 - KINDERPLAY

It was time to take on the big guys in the 'educational toys' supply business. Through Helen's contacts, I set out on a survey of kindergartens and play centres as to where and what supplies they purchased regularly.

The plan was to set up a retail outlet and have a wholesale supply division to sell directly to kindergartens, primary schools, play centres, and specialty toy libraries. I needed to thoroughly research my suppliers and potential competition. The more I researched, the more opportunities screamed out to me, 'Do It.'

Early in 1974 I rented a small shop at the top of the hill at 834 Burke Road, Camberwell.

My brother-in-law, Rob completed the fit out on a shoestring budget. I'd set the merchandise categories to cover infants to primary school kids.

Most toyshops were sourcing their entire stock from the same half dozen toy wholesalers.

My selection of art materials alone came from 10 different wholesalers. I wanted Kinderplay to be a standout supplier of quality playthings, and it was. I had the best range of children's musical instruments possible, and not one item sourced from the toy trade. We also stocked a specialised selection of children's books.

I employed a staff of one, and purchased a Renault station wagon, yes, another Renault, as our delivery vehicle.

You'd think I'd have chosen a more suitable vehicle, this time. I sent out a letter of introduction to kindergartens and primary schools in the eastern suburbs, stocked up the wagon, and hit the road. We soon outgrew the Camberwell location, and I took a lease on a much bigger shop at 1044 High Street, Armadale.

Again Rob completed the fit out, and we kicked arse. Our merchandise range expanded to include kindergarten furniture.

After a few years there, we outgrew these premises and moved to a much more modern building at 1032-4 High Street where Kinderplay is still located as I write.

I upgraded the vehicle to a Toyota Hi Ace van, and employed a very competent

Gary Eaton to handle the roadwork. He was a very disciplined, organised, if somewhat pedantic fellow who stayed with me for many years.

One of my most important local suppliers was Konrad Asto, a Swiss trained cabinet maker, who designed and manufactured a wonderful range high of quality wooden toys.

He also made our painting easels, blackboards and kindergarten tables, chairs and book display shelves.

The standard of Konrad's work matched his eagerness to be the best in his field. We partnered to design and manufacture a range of 'instant reward' toys for children with learning disabilities. We worked with Noah's Ark Toy Library and a number of specialty schools, to test and evaluate our prototype creations.

Kinderplay's specialty 'toy' range was used at the very challenging, St. Nicholas Hospital, in Carlton.

We received very useful feedback from Rosemary Crossley, an expert in facilitated communication for non-verbal people. We provided a number of instant reward items that appear in the 1984 film, *Annie's Coming Out*.

European Holiday Break

Kinderplay was pretty full on and prior to starting a family Helen and I planned an overseas holiday. We travelled through the UK, France, Belgium, Germany and Holland. On the European leg we shared a beaten-up, gerry-built Thames camper van as our method of transport, with another couple. They had bought the van from backpacking Aussies out the front of Australia House, in London. It proved to be a six-hundred-quid lemon.

Rhonda, who used to work for me at Kinderplay and Ross (her husband) had been travelling in the van for many months before we joined them. They were a totally hilarious couple to travel with, but they were uproariously disorganised; plus Ross stuttered badly. The more pressure he was under, the worse the stammer.

When we set off from the UK to France the weather was starting to chill down, somewhat. We drove down to Dover and on to the giant hovercraft to Calais on the French side of the English Channel.

We experienced an incredibly rough crossing. Not at all for the faint hearted.

Ross insisted on being the first driver for this venture in Europe. He drove the old van off the hovercraft and we cleared customs. Next stop, Paris. Ross commented on how friendly the locals were; all waving at us. Maybe it was the Aussie sticker on the front-bumper-mounted spare tyre?

No. We were driving on the wrong side of the road.

We couldn't all sleep in the van, so Helen and I would stay at B&Bs or cheap hostels or hotels. Some nights we had to sneak our friends into our digs so they could shower or whatever.

On the border crossing going into Belgium the guard asked for our passports and international drivers licence. Ross couldn't find either and the more annoyed the guard became the worse the stammering grew. In the end the officer just waved us through muttering 'stupid Australians'. It was a memorable trip and really recharged our batteries...ready to Kinderplay to the next step.

Tokyo Toy Fair

A Sydney supplier had advised me that Japan was making great inroads into children's toys and construction sets. As I was keen to keep my point of difference, I set off to the Tokyo toy fair. I had no idea how business was conducted in this part of the world. I travelled there with a Sydney supplier, John Simmons. He was about six feet four tall, had blue eyes and blonde hair; that's something the Japanese people rarely see, if ever.

John informed me that we had to buy via a local agent, and he set me up with a contact. John explained that cultural norms assert that you couldn't just rock up at a toy fair in Japan, and expect to place an order.

So much to learn.

My budget hotel room at Ueno (Tokyo) was tiny, with barely enough room to change my mind. The hotel breakfast experience in the overcrowded dining room didn't work for me. The food looked most unappetising and I detested the slurping noises. I still can't abide noisy eaters. I also can't stand anyone talking with food in their mouth. Sorry.

The toy trade fair was amazing, and I was in the import business in no time. This helped Kinderplay maintain a real point of difference to other retailers. That's the goal, point of difference, plus quality, price points and a workable profit margin. I told my retail mates that I only worked on a 3% profit margin. Buy at $1 sell at $3. That has to work!

I visited Japan many times over the next decade.

The other great world toy fairs were held in Hong Kong, Germany and the U.K.

In 1978 Richard Opat and I did the big overseas business trip together. Richard was in the schmutter business and was a partner in a number of women's clothing retail stores. (He was very big in women's clothing.)

Our first port of call was Hong Kong. The trade fair there was interesting, and that's deliberately a weak description.

Business aside, it was great fun. We stayed in a very fancy hotel at budget rates. They even served breakfast in the rooms, on a white linen tablecloth, at any time of day.

Everywhere we went we were assumed to be partners…and I'm not talking business partners.

"A twin room, please".

"We understand, gentlemen".

"Excuse me, but the room only has a double bed".

"We understand, gentlemen".

Lowering my voice an octave, I'd add, "No you don't understand. Richard and I are both married to two different women and we each have children in tow. We are mates. Best mates but NOT bedroom mates".

Next stop was England, where the IRA set off a fireworks display to welcome us.

The Irish Republican Army was creating havoc in London, and we soon became aware of the 'no go' areas.

Richard went off and did his thing while I attended the British Toy Fair.

I was particularity taken by Galt Toys, the ultimate range of educational playthings for me, at that time.

Over the next five years I imported an extensive range of superb items from this company, established in Manchester in 1836. Another range I imported was from Casden Toys. We had huge success with their products. Today, Casden items pop up in Aldi stores. Most if not all items are now manufactured in China.

What a pity!

For me, the ultimate toy fair was the Nuremberg Spiel Warren Messer. Richard was uncomfortable about visiting this region at the time, so he went off to Holland. Nuremberg Toy Fair took over the whole city accommodation wise. This was the largest trade fair of its type in Europe, and I had to take a room in a local family home. My hosts didn't speak English (or chose not to) for the six days I was billeted with them.

Thankfully, by the day's end I was exhausted and after a meal (served in my room) I completed my paperwork, and went to bed. It was a very uncomfortable homestay and, thankfully, I was able to leave a day earlier than planned. I had an arrangement to meet Richard in Paris. He was coming in from Holland, and I wasn't sure if he would already be there. We had booked a room in an old, established hotel, a little off the tourist track. He didn't know I was coming a day earlier than planned. We both travelled by train and had no need to pre-book our travel through Europe.

I checked in and was told that Richard had arrived the previous day. I was given a key to our large, twin room on the fourth floor. Richard was always very organised and I could see from his diary notes on the desk that he was out visiting a museum nearby.

I locked the door from the inside, had a catnap, and waited. Eventually, I heard the key turning but not allowing the door to open.

He's a patient fellow, is Rick. Next, I hear him trying to explain to an impatient housekeeper that the door won't open...in French. He doesn't speak French and the housekeeper didn't, or more likely, wouldn't speak English. They summoned a housemaid; meanwhile I unlocked the door on my side and jumped back on my bed. The maid had no trouble gaining entry. They all peered in and I asked, "What seems to be the problem"?

Paris was also hosting a rather small toy trade fair, which was a good enough excuse for us adding this magnificent city to our itinerary.

Back home in Melbourne I could hardly wait for the unique ranges of imported stock to arrive at the shop.

I had between four and six staff at this point, and everyone was so excited to open the cartons containing children's products they had not seen anywhere. The shop took on a new buzz. I always encouraged our customers to share the enthusiasm.

On a subsequent buying trip to Japan, after visiting my regular suppliers, I was introduced to a range of fairly expensive, extremely hi-tech, radio-controlled toys. I bought a few 'one off' items. I thought these would attract a good deal of interest in the window displays, and I could have a little play, too. I took one of the fancy radio-controlled aeroplanes to the park near home for a test flight. There was no one around when I managed to get the plane airborne. The test flight went well until a passing taxi made a radio call.

The plane responded to this radio frequency intrusion by crash landing.

Legendary ABC Radio National presenter Phillip Adams purchased the very fancy hydrofoil boat that I had displayed in the window. His vessel also suffered a few radio control issues, too. He sent me a beautifully crafted letter stating that in his opinion, it came as no surprise that the hi-tech boat was shaped somewhat like a suppository. He made some suggestions regarding the vessel that could have turned out to be very painful to this innocent vendor.

Bankcard

A very smartly dressed, hatted woman came to the shop to introduce me to Bankcard. This little piece of plastic fantastic, launched by then Prime Minister Gough Whitlam in 1974, would allow our customers to buy on credit.

The deal was that a customer buys a $10 item and hands over their plastic card. I manually swipe the card against a paper slip, in a merchant machine. The customer gets a copy, I get a copy and I bank a copy, with a merchant summary of the day's bankcard sales. A few days later, my $10 is now worth $9.50 and that's what appears in my bank. "So, there is extra paperwork and a delay in a depleted payment?" I asked. She went on to tell me that if the sale was above our allocated floor limit, I would need to phone up for an authorisation number. 'Hello'!

I deferred accepting bankcard until it was well established and their commission rate dropped to 3.5%. The positive result was that customers were not using lay-by so much, and made larger purchases with ease.

While our children's book selection expanded, the range of worthwhile children's music on vinyl and compact cassette was, to say the least, wanting.

Listen To The Band

As I'd had many years experience with traditional jazz bands, I decided to produce a series of children's recordings introducing different music styles to very young children.

Volume one, naturally, had to be trad jazz. I wanted to use a female vocalist to introduce the instruments in the band. The band was to build up track by track. I assembled a group of totally wonderful musicians for this project. I played in the initial sessions as I tried out a few vocalists.

The standout was folk singer, Shirley Jacobs. She was a colourful character and thoroughly professional.

Shirley was married to convicted gangster, Joey Hamilton and she did tell me that at times her life was at risk from some of his connections. The bullet holes in the back of her car were real.

Shirley was a highly respected musician who collaborated with many famous jazz musicians, including Ade Monsbourgh, on a number of recordings. We really hit it off and Shirley Jacobs was a pleasure to work with.

As the project was coming together I made the easy decision to replace myself as trumpet player and bandleader, and concentrate on the production side.

I appointed Richard Miller (clarinet and xylophone) as musical director and Ian

Orr on trumpet. I already had Chris Farley (banjo), Bill Morris (tuba and kinder bells) and, of course, Richard Opat (drums, percussion and gumboots*).

Richard Miller took over the musical arrangements and added Roger Jane (trombone). Incidentally, Richard drove an old Citroen that featured little cardboard flap he had installed on the dashboard. I enquired as to what's under the flap. "A digital clock, and I loathe digital displays", he advised. This fine musician (he practises every day) went on to play with The Red Onions and The Society Syncopators, largely due to fine leadership with the Kinderplay Allstars, I suspect.

The choice of recording studio was very easy for me. I had produced an album, titled 'Rejoice, and Sing' with the Le Masurier Quartet, in October 1975, at Bruce Adderly Sound Studios, in West Melbourne. This was the favoured venue. Some recording engineers tended to be a little precious: not Bruce. He had total control of the multi-track, analogue recording system and the experience to cope with whatever the session threw up. Bruce liked to work long and late, and looked like he hadn't seen too much daylight over the past few years. He's still doing what he loves best, all these forty plus years later.

Listen To The Band! (Volume 1)

Shirley Jacobs with the Kinderplay Allstars was recorded in one session, with a few overdubs a day later. (*Richard Opat had to count in 'Sally's Galoshes' using gumboots in a Kinderplay sand and water play tray.)

The album (JBP 7608*) sold thousands of copies on vinyl and cassette.

John Bye Productions 1976:08

I personally delivered copies of the record to a number of radio stations, hoping for some airplay. The only one to play the album was 3LO (ABC Melbourne). The late, great Peter Evans presented the breakfast program, and was such a marvellous support, as was the morning presenter, Mary Adams. Thank you, ABC.

For the album launch I hired Malvern Town Hall and had Shirley and the Kinderplay Allstars perform live on stage. We packed the hall with kids from infants to seven year olds (and their parents).

Then followed,

Listen To The Band! (Volume 2)

Ronnie Burns and the Kinderplay Rockets. (JBP 7709)

This had to be a rock band again building up as the album progressed. For balance I wanted a male singer. I approached Ronnie Burns, who had been one of the few local rock stars who seemed to totally have his act together. Helen and I were living in Service Street, Hampton, by now, and we had our first rehearsal there. It wasn't great and I had a few issues with the tune selection and the musician mix wasn't right. Ronnie wasn't totally comfortable. We had a preproduction luncheon at Ronnie's home and agreed to tweak the settings.

I made the necessary, ever-so-slight line-up changes and again appointed Richard Miller as musical director. Together we collected an amazing group of top class musicians to form

'Ronnie Burns and The Kinderplay Rockettes'.

Check out this lineup:

Bob Sedergreen, Laurie Ralph, Richard Miller, Peter Hocking, Ian Mason and Tom Cowburn.

The studio session was absolutely amazing. Ronnie was a one-take-wonder; a true professional. Again, Bruce Adderly performed his analogue magic and we had a great record.

Amazingly, volume three fell into production with a minimum of stress. I was very impressed with Melbournes #1 bush band 'The Cobbers' and they were keen to record with my little label. The result was...

Listen To The Band! (Volume 3)

Cobbers, the Bonza Bush Band. (JBP 7808)

Australian bush band music at its best! This is a frolicking romp with Christy Cooney, Mark Brown, John Armstrong, Bruce Cawthorne and Chris Armstrong.

All three LTTB albums were recorded at BASS, West Melbourne.

Thanks Bruce.

I became obsessed with tracking down the best children's albums I could find. The best of the best came out of Canada. The artist simply known as Raffi headed up a gentle, versatile band and I continued to import and distribute his albums in Australia for many, many years.

Local children's entertainer, Franciscus Henri, had a number of very fine recordings, and I became his distributor for a time.

I also produced an album with Franc, titled

'Sunshine, Rainbows and Violins' (JBP 8108)

We held the album launch in the front window of Kinderplay and at the Malvern town hall.

I sent a copy of 'Sunshine, Rainbows and Violins' to Raffi, and he covered one of Franc's original songs.

The following year I recorded a Christmas Album with Franciscus Henri and a few of my favourite muso mates. We recorded this in the tiny studio at Dex Audio, in Spencer Street, West Melbourne.

The plan was a limited release on cassette only, but it was later released by Move Records on CD. It's a delightful little recording.

Dex Audio was my choice for all cassette duplication.

Interestingly, my catalogue number allocation was JBP 8108 (John Bye Productions) and the year of release. 'Funny how they all came out ahead of the Christmas season sales build up.

Meanwhile at Kinderplay the kindergarten supply side of the business was now well established and attracted a number of copycats. I was getting feedback from a few suppliers that questions were being asked about the way Kinderplay sourced product.

I always kept my cards close to my chest but I was ready for a new challenge.

During our Kinderplay decade, Helen and I moved from Mooroolbark to Hampton and back to Blackburn. We brought three little girls into the world. The first on the scene was Kylie-Ann while we were living in Mooroolbark in 1976. Given that Helen's birthday is Jan 1st and mine is Jan 4th, why she chose Jan 5th is still a mystery. We moved to Hampton and in 1980 Katie turned up on June 11th. She was't going toe the line and rock up in January. She wasn't going to toe any line; and that's that. As Helen had experienced a very dangerous ectopic pregnancy, we were advised by one of Melbourne's leading obstetrician-gynaecologist, Lorna Lloyd-Green CBE, that our family was most likely complete. Katie blew that theory up.

Then, eighteen months later (December 15th) Emily turned up. Dr Lloyd Green said she was as amazed as we were and asked me what name we had in mind for this new little person. I said that I fancied the name 'Lorna Lloyd Bye'.

Around 1983 we bought a little beach house on Phillip Island. It was ever-so-slightly run down and when it rained we all got wet. Rob and I (O.K. Rob) replaced the roof and built a verandah at the front. The house was in a very quiet, safe street and our three little girls were allowed to play free range, provided they all stayed together.

We had a small population of koalas around our area and from time to time tourists would wander about hoping to get a nice photo of the little fellows.

Our holiday house neighbour was a plumber with a huge extension ladder. I had access to very realistic, life size-toy koalas. Now, join the dots and you can guess what happened next.

Many tourists left the Island with pics of 'Cyril, The Stuffed'.

Time was unkind to Cyril, and over the years he looked less and less like the real thing.

We also had a stuffed toy wombat that I pulled along with some fishing line. It kept falling over and fooled no one.

The girls thought it was hilarious seeing their dad acting like a big, silly kid.

Kaite (left), Emily and Kylie-Ann.

My daughter Kylie-Ann (left) with her little mate, Caroline. They remain great friends as are their daughters.

Richards's son, Andrew

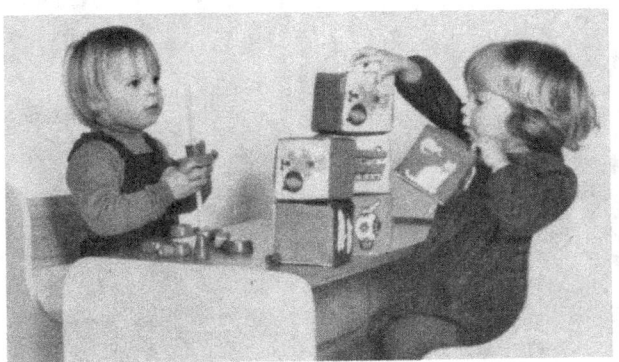

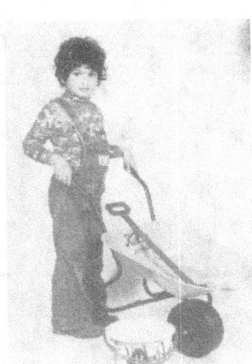

Catalogue front cover, bottom left is my daughter Katie. My youngest daughter, Emily, was just a baby and missed this print run. Sorry Em.

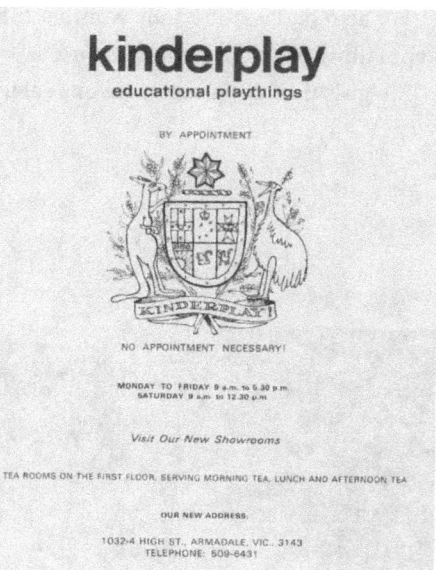

Listen the Band Vol 1
Burce Adderkey and I in the control room

Sunshine, Rainbows and Violins
Michael Letho at York Studio

Chris Farley (left) and Shirley Jacobs at the Malvern Town Hall record launch

Listen the Band Vol 2

Richard Miller   *Ronnie Burns*   *Bob Sedergreen*

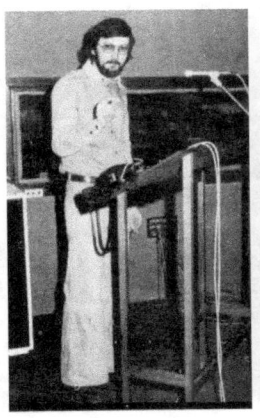

Listen the Band Vol 3: Cobbers ... the bonza bush band

L-R: Mark Brown, John Armstrong, Christy Cooney   *L-R: Bruce Cawthorne, John Armstrong*

Neil Orchard   *Kylie-Ann and Franciscus*

Richard Opat   *Greg O'Leary*   *Greg Hilderbrand*   *Philip Gardner*

20 - JOHN BYE PRODUCTIONS

While recording various jazz and children's records I realised that my talent as a musician was much more appreciated if I didn't literally blow my own trumpet. I was much better at organising far more talented players and putting projects together. I had my own outlet for the children's recordings and I continued supplying outlets Australia wide.

My idea was to expand my production company as succession planning. Post Kinderplay I saw myself as a record producer, importer and distributor of children's records.

In the early eighties, one of my favourite bands around Melbourne was 'New Harlem'. This band was formed and led by Ian Smith, who is still very well represented in so many iconic Melbourne jazz combos.

Ian started out as a trumpet player and can still be found around the traps playing trumpet, drums, sousaphone or whatever he chooses, but not at the same time. He was the go-to man who has assembled bands to accompany or entertain many famous identities including The King of Thailand and Spike Milligan (both of whom were competent trumpet players).

I knew all the New Harlem guys pretty well, and I'd often drop in to Athol's Abbey at the Casa de Manana Hotel (aka 'Case Of Bananas') to hear them play. Down the track, after Smithy had moved on, I approached the band with the view to making a live album. They were very keen and I began preproduction arrangements. The 'Abbey' was not a suitable recording venue.

The tune selection was up to the band.

Bruce Adderly Studios was the right setting for such a recording and Bruce and I had worked on many projects there.

My plan was to record the album in one session with an invited audience in the studio. I wasn't sure that the 'live' album was going to work so, on the night, I asked the audience to pause for 3 seconds before applauding. That way I could decide post production what worked better. When recording 'live' it's difficult to do a second and perhaps, third take, but 'live' adds an edgy excitement factor. Also, false starts are less likely. As the audience was made up of our collective friends, they totally co-operated. The session was flawless except that Sandro Donati fluffed one high note on 'Just A Gigolo'.

We didn't pick it up until the mix the next day. Sandro came in to the studio and just recorded that one note. Bruce cut and pasted on the trumpet track, and the magic worked. Sorry Sandro, but you were great to work with and a marvellous vocalist.

We recorded this album on Ampex 2" 24-track analogue equipment. Today most studios use digital 'Pro Tools' programs (or similar) and track separation is much more sophisticated. This does NOT necessarily make for better recordings. Two-inch magnetic tape was very expensive whilst digital storage is as cheap as chips; literally!

'New Harlem Live Before A Recorded Audience' (YPRX 1890 through EMI)
Recorded at Bruce Adderly Sound Studios on August 3rd 1981

How's this for a fine group of musos?
Chris Ludowyk, Bob Gilbert, Sandro Donati, Neil Orchard, Chris Farley,
Bill Morris and, here he is again…Richard Opat.

Famed Melbourne artist, Roland Harvey created the most wonderful cover with the band performing to a cardboard cutout audience. I had a prearranged distribution agreement with EMI subject to approval of the final masters. They absolutely loved the sound and the concept.

I now had a major manufacturer and distribution company on side. We achieved reasonable airplay, but commercial radio was totally uninterested. Disappointing? I'll say.

No surprise that I love the ABC and the many community radio stations.
Thankfully, community radio is going from strength to strength in Australia.

Vince Jones

After the New Harlem recording session one of the guys suggested we go down to Lygon Street, Carlton, to unwind. At the Parachute Club a fresh young vocalist had a gig with some of the Channel Nine musicians, kicking off at about 11 pm. 'Why not'? I thought. About six of us arrived at the venue above a restaurant in the strip, to see an uncomfortable young guy in an ill-fitting suit, singing his heart out.

Everyone patron in the room was spellbound. Even the backing band members glanced at each other in wonderment. I had never witnessed such a gifted performance, albeit a little uncomfortable to watch.

The vocalist appeared a touch awkward in his movements, but his delivery was pitch perfect.

It wasn't until the second set that I heard his name mentioned.

I didn't know at that time that Vince Jones was to be my next recording artist. I approached him during a break and he waved me away with "talk to my manager, man".

I wasn't easily put off, so I did just that.

Marc Gonsalves (aka Marc Gunn) who was the Saturday morning jazz presenter at PBSFM was Vince's manager. Incidentally, to this very day, I hold up PBSFM as Australia's greatest radio station.

I'd met Marc at PBS when the studios were in Fitzroy Street, St Kilda, so he sort of knew me.

It was about 1:30 am when we agreed to meet up later in the week to discuss making an album for Vince.

Marc was a great jazz radio presenter but a complicated fellow, and I didn't feel he had the skills to handle the very difficult, amazingly talented, Vince Jones. Marc gave me a copy of a demo (cassette) tape that Vince had made at Dex Audio. It was a rather impressive recording, but nothing eventuated, album wise.

The recording engineer was Daniel Desiere, one of the directors of Dex Audio. Daniel had questionable people skills, but he was an exceptionally fine recording engineer. Vince had total confidence in Daniel so there's a positive!

The Dex Audio recording studio in Spencer Street, West Melbourne, was tiny and not suitable for my proposed first ever Vince Jones album. This is prior to Dex Audio establishing Newmarket Recording Studios in Arden Street, North Melbourne, where I went on to make many albums.

I had a very good relationship with Dex Audio who duplicated my children's cassettes . Co-founders, Greg Williams and Daniel Desiere and I have worked on many projects over decades. I really admire these guys' technical skills. Daniel had a photographic memory for circuit board troubleshooting. Truly amazing!

It was clear that Daniel was to be the recording engineer on Vince's first album. The band lineup was Vince's call and Russell Smith (remember him from my Lake's Entrance story?) was appointed musical producer. The studio was to be

Richmond Recorders, where Greg and Daniel had been involved in upgrading the recording equipment. As executive producer I set the dates and booked the studio for three sessions in November 1981. Three sessions at a major recording studio plus session rates for all associated amounted to a huge commitment for me. I did have a few sleepless nights over this project. I was well aware that a large percentage of Australian jazz albums fail dismally to recover costs, but I did have faith in Vince and all the musicians and crew.

We had a midday bump in (setup) and recording commenced at about 3 pm.

Day one was amazing. Vince was in fine voice and his musicians lifted to a new level. The band featured Doug De Vries, Mart (Jex) Saarelht, Mike Williams, Peter Blick and Alex Pertout.

After the first session I took a cassette copy of the unmixed tracks home, and sat up half the night with my headphones on, beaming with delight. I knew this was a very special recording in the making.

Day two. Setup again. We had a very special guest organised to accompany Vince on 'As Time Goes By'.

The legendary pianist Ron Rosenberg (GTV 9) had agreed to provide the solo accompaniment. He arrived at the appointed time, but...no Vince.

Ron wasn't happy, but eventually our hero returned.

'Vince, what's the story?' I asked. He explained that he caught the tram down to Brashs' electrical store to buy some cassettes that were on sale. Ron was unimpressed. I was unimpressed and hundreds of dollars of studio time later, Vince and Ron gave an amazing performance of this classic tune. All was forgiven.

Our sessions had to finish at 12:00 a.m. as another band had the studio booked from midnight to daylight.

That band was 'Men At Work'. They achieved world wide fame with their 'Land Down Under' track.

'Watch What Happens' Vince Jones (YPRX 1933)

John Bye Productions through EMI Australia came out in 1982 to critical acclaim. The team at EMI were very impressed.

I arranged an official launch in March 1982, at The Grain Store Tavern, in King Street, Melbourne. I had the all kazoo 'Glenn Lautrec Little Big Band' (Red Faces finalists) booked as the warm up act. The house was packed. Vince wanted to open the set with a tune that wasn't on the album. I tried to calmly explain that at an album launch, you play the tunes on the recording. It's not rocket science, but Vince was just plain DIFFICULT.

'Watch What Happens' was acclaimed in The Age newspaper (24th April 1982) as 'Critics Choice'. In late 1982 Mike Daly listed in the top jazz albums of the year. Adrian Jackson of Jazz magazine touted Jones as the "new Melbourne jazz star" in June 1982.

The Sydney based JAZZ Music Magazine (May/June 1982) ran a four page feature on 'Watch What Happens' and the arrival of Vince Jones suggesting he was Melbourne's new jazz star. Editor, Eric Myers, also posed the question, is Vince Jones the new Billy Field? Vince was not happy about such an undertone. Eric sent me a copy of the magazine with an accompanying letter stating that he "had enormous difficulty in getting a modicum of co-operation from Marc Gunn". He went on to question his artist management skills. At the time Eric Myers was also the jazz critic for the Sydney Morning Herald.

Vince and Marc soon parted company.

I sent a copy of the album to Allan Zavod (my Bay City pianist) who had hit the 'big league' and was regularly touring America with the Duke Ellington Orchestra. He was also composing film scores in Hollywood.

He had subsequently toured with Frank Zappa. Allan loved the record and suggested the we could get together and discuss putting a tour together for Vince. He sure had the contacts to make things happen, big time. I ran the idea past Vince who showed less than no interest. I did say he was difficult.

The man's vocal talent was unsurpassed and I became determined to take up the challenge and make a second album despite the unnecessary stumbling blocks Vince managed to throw up.

This second album had a new line-up. Doug De Vries on guitar was the only band member on both albums. Who would have guessed?

The new line-up included Allan Browne, Mark Fitzgibbon, Hermann Schwaiger and Peter Jones.

Russell Smith stayed on as musical producer, but Vince wanted to change studios and recording engineer.

This time it was the much more Ritzy, and expensive, A.A.V. studios in South Melbourne, with acclaimed sound engineer Ross Cockle.

The special guest on the title track was Wilbur Wilde on tenor sax.

Wilbur played three takes of his solo piece, and the difficulty was choosing which one to use. All three were amazing.

"Spell' Vince Jones (YPRX 2078)

John Bye Productions through EMI Australia

'Spell' is a great recording but trying to get Vince Jones and his ever-changing management to co-operate was like herding cats. He was just too precious to persevere with.

After this second album, I decided...no more Vince for me.

There's an old jazz standard titled 'Have You Met Miss Jones?'

Around the traps they say 'Have You Left Vince Jones?' I totally understand that.

I sold the rights of these first two albums to Vince and his new manager in April 1984.

He re-released them without any mention of his executive producer. I think that says it all. I took the financial risk and I put so much on the line for this fellow. Thanks Vince.

He went on to a new parallel career as a jazz vocalist and a born again green ambassador. He'd lecture his audience on how they should cut down on their wasteful excesses, while he flew his little aeroplane around to gigs across the country! This was a huge turnoff for his audiences.

If ever the musicians and support crew whom Vince sacked over the years decided to have a reunion, they'd need to hire the Melbourne Town Hall. Having said all that, I saw him perform recently and he was in fine form.

Another course change

While all this was happening, Kinderplay was at its peak, and I had a party keen to purchase the business.

I was ready for a change. The timing was perfect and Kinderplay passed on to new owners.

I rented an office in Camberwell and concentrated on children's music for a period. It was like having a gap year really. Meanwhile, David Glat, who owned a toyshop in Elsternwick, told me he too wanted to sell out.

I connected him with Gary Eaton, who had worked for me at Kinderplay. Gary bought 'Child and Adult' and ran that business for about thirty years.

By now David was at a loose end and I was ready for a new project.

David introduced me to a colleague, Alex Bryla. He'd been in the novelty electronics import business and struck me as a pretty smart operator, in an Arthur Daley sort of way. I liked the positive vibe Alex projected. We enjoyed a few long lunches, and yes, I was known as 'Sir Lunchalot'.

During one of these meetings we came up with the idea of an overseas fact-finding trip, much like our politicians enjoy, with the obvious exception that they use the public purse.

The plan was to check out retail stores in the stationery, gift and/or novelty areas. We also had one eye on the photo processing systems that were springing up around the marketplace. These were the times when you'd take your exposed camera film down to the local chemist, and pick up your grossly expensive 12 or 24 (6 X 4) glossy photographs a week later. The cost of the develop/print equipment was falling but the margins were going north.

In 1983 David, Alex and I had mobile phones fitted in our cars. They were incredibly expensive to install and use, but we thought we were cool, young guys going somewhere. Alex's carphone was worth more than his car. My first call was from Helen asking me to bring some milk home.

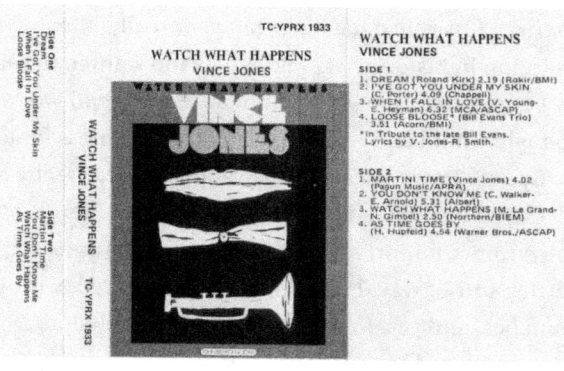

The Age Weekender, 8th April 1982

VINCE JONES QUINTET "Watch What Happens" John Bye Productions, thru EMI (YPRX 1933). Melbourne jazz singer Vince Jones has won a lot of fans with his stylish approach, and he'll win a lot more with this excellent debut LP. His singing is brilliant, both impressive and appealing, and the playing is superb, with pianist Mark Saarelaht, guitarist Doug DeBries and Jones (on trumpet or flugelhorn) being featured. The album brilliantly captures what Jones is all about. There isn't a bad track, but if you need convincing, try the definitive version of 'As Time Goes By'.
— Adrian Jackson

The Age Saturday Extra, 1st January 1983

Michael Daly and Michael Shmith choose the best releases of 1982.

crisp sound round out a fine Australian production.

WATCH WHAT HAPPENS — Vince Jones (John Bye Productions, through EMI, YPRX 1933): a polished performance that will come as no surprise to those who have heard this Melbourne-based jazz singer-trumpeter and his group. The Jones boy can swing or scat with the greatest of ease, and deliver a ballad with a maturity that belies his 27 years. The two ballads are outstanding — a superb rendition of Nat King Cole's 'When I Fall In Love', and a virtuoso performance of 'As Time Goes By' that makes you forget how many times you heard it before.

NIGHT & DAY — Joe Jackson (A&M L 37857): a remarkable achievement that steps neatly between jazz, swing, salsa, electro-pop and ballads. Jackson has always been a sharp songsmith, acquiring greater sophistication with each new record, but he will find it hard to surpass his latest effort. He plays an array of keyboards and percussion, plus alto sax, sings and arranges, backed by percussionists and rhythm players. 'Real Men' is a real gem, 'Stepping Out' is contemporary and bursting with optimism, and 'A Slow Song' makes a plea for low-energy music, with a tasty bridging organ solo.

THE CONCERTS IN CHINA — Jean Michel Jarre (Polydor 2612 039): a double-LP souvenir of Jarre's spectacular concert tour of China last year. The experience must have overwhelmed the Peking and Shanghai audiences, unused to the sheer technological power of an electronic rock band. Highlight of the set is 'Souvenir Of China', which blends everyday sounds recorded during his stay, spliced with the sound of a clicking camera lens and a haunting musical theme.

THE NYLON CURTAIN — Billy Joel (CBS SBP 237821): the piano man takes

'Watch What Happens' album cover notes

WATCH WHAT HAPPENS

is a most appropriate title for this first album by the still developing talent of Vincent Jones, coming as it does early in 1982 which began so auspiciously for Vince with his week-long appearance at the Festival of Perth.

There he worked in brilliant company — giants like Freddie Hubbard, Keith Jarrett and Chick Corea, Cleo Laine and John Dankworth — and with his pianist Mart Saarelaht combining with the trio of brilliant British guitarist John Etheridge to form a quintet.

However, Vince Jones is used to moving in WHO'S WHO company. In 1981 his quintet was the support for the Melbourne concerts by Oscar Petersen and his trio. That success led to the Vince Jones Quintet being booked for later tours by the Pointer Sisters and tenorist Joe Henderson.

So, who is Vince Jones?

He is a very gifted young musician and a notable addition to the list of distinguished Australian artists. Born in Scotland in 1955, Vince moved with his family to Australia in 1965, settling in Wollongong, N.S.W.

His introduction to jazz came at an early age when, back in Glasgow, he listened on his father's knee to radio broadcasts of Charlie 'Bird' Parker, Miles Davis, Sonny Rollins and Dizzy Gillespie, to name but a few. It was the music of these great craftsmen that drew Vince closer to jazz.

Essentially a self-taught musician, Vince besides singing also plays trumpet and flugelhorn. I first heard his quintet at a small venue in Carlton, Melbourne, a year ago and soon joined his band of enthusiastic, discriminating and devoted followers.

Opening these notes I appraised this young artist's talent as "still developing", and later recorded my belief in his giftedness. Develop he will because of his gift of innate musicianship.

As a singer, his range is extensive and he uses it tellingly and tastefully. His pitch is true and his time so sure for such a melismatic singer. His trumpet and flugelhorn pleases with every hearing.

Vince Jones is one of a rare and wonderful breed of jazz singers — a natural musician with the ability to become one of the greatest. He is strongly supported on this recording by his fellow musicians — in particular guitarist Doug De Vries and pianist Mart Saarelaht.

I find this album delightful and so satisfyingly musical... and with it Vince Jones makes a most impressive debut as a recording artist.

Ian M. Neil (Music To Midnight)

VINCE JONES: Vocals, Trumpet, Flugelhorn
Mart Saarelaht: Piano
Doug De Vries: Guitar
Mike Williams: Fender Bass
Peter Blick: Drums
Alex Pertout: Percussion
Special thanks to Ron Rosenberg (Piano on As Time Goes By)

Produced by: Russell Smith
Engineered by: Daniel Desiere
Engineering Assistant: Greg Williams
Production Co-ordinator: Marc Gunn
Executive Producer: John Bye
Recorded at Richmond Recorders, November 81.

Cover Art: D. Walker   Layout: Hocking Graphics

21 - GUESS WHAT?

Our fact-finding tour included Hong Kong, Japan and the USA.

Everywhere we went we visited the large malls, the grungy side streets and the trendy strip retailers.

From very Ritzy shopping centres in Hong Kong and Tokyo to trendy little gift shops down side streets we'd make notes and take pics. We timed our arrival into Los Angeles to allow us to visit the Californian gift-trade fare. Typically of Alex, he managed to use our newly registered 'travel business' to book us into a very nice hotel in Beverley Hills. After a full day at the trade fair it was rather enjoyable to return to such classy accommodation and enjoy dining in style. On our second evening there I was thrilled to hear that a modern jazz quartet were to perform after dinner. During a break I had a chat to the pianist who, on picking my accent, told me his piano teacher was Australian. 'Really, who would that be?' I enquired. When I told him that I too, have played with Allan Zavod, I got that 'yeah, yeah look. 'So', he said, 'if I get Allan on my cellphone now, he'll know who you are'? He did and he did!

I told Allan that I was in town with two associates and he insisted we all jump in a cab and come to his place, immediately. We did. What an amazing experience we were in for! The big, open-plan house was in the Hollywood hills not far from the famous sign. It had a well equipped bandstand centrally located in the huge living area.

We arrived well after midnight and the place was jumping. Musos were rocking up after their gigs, for a jam session and perhaps a little something extra on the side. Allan was in fine form and made us most welcome. He always made time to make everyone feel special. He was generous, outgoing and never played 'the star'. We stayed for a couple of hours but it was certainly not our scene. Some of his guests were so untidy that they'd left traces of talcum powder all over the bathroom bench. I've strayed from my comfort zone quite a few times but this elevated the experience to a whole new level.

Around Los Angeles was a chain of giftware stores titled 'Ahhs!' They really caught our attention. These were very trendy shops with lots of neon signage, selling novelty giftware, stationery and clothing. High energy, always busy stores in hi-vis locations. These very impressive retail outlets stayed open well after other shops closed. The downside was that we didn't have access to anything close to this product range
in Australia, and the cost of setting up same would have been totally prohibitive.

The famous San Francisco tourist trap, Pier 39, had a marvellous range of cool shops. I took lots of photos of the displays and shop fittings. As photos were not usually permitted in the stores, I'd pretend to take pics of David and Alex. An exaggerated broad Aussie accent usually tamed the angry shopkeeper. We did get some good marketing and product sourcing ideas in the USA and we came up with our brand name.

Riding on an escalator in New York, we spotted a name on a perfectly modelled pair of jeans, with a 'GUESS' patch ideally placed.

Guess What? Yes, that's it!

Alex had a great contact in Japan, who was a freelance buyers' agent. Harry San knew the ropes and in Japan you need an agent. This market was totally unique and giftware stores also sold exquisite stationery and novel confectionery items. Gifts were beautifully wrapped; often with an added brightly coloured candy stick.

We had never seen stores like these before. We timed our Japanese visit to coincide with the Tokyo gift fair.

Back in Melbourne we formulated a plan to open three stores selling 'essential non-essentials'. We collated all the photos, advertising material and all the product info we collected overseas. We registered the business name "Guess What?", and researched suitable locations.

In the early eighties prime retail space was scarce in the better shopping strips, and very expensive. The prime locations could demand 'key money'. That's buying a lease, before you commence! We were not in that league. While the sites search went on, we planned the product mix and the shop fittings required. I had my office in Camberwell, where we had plenty of room to work.

We had all our fittings made for us by Robert (my brother-in-law) and Konrad (my toy manufacturer) plus a couple of other talented young guys. Our shop fittings and display stands were a combination of the best ideas we came across overseas. The pink and grey 'ice-cream cart' shelving units made our stores look unique and quirky.

Our proposed product range meant we all had to get out and track down suppliers who don't fit into the mainstream giftware trade. There was a whole range of items we dreamt up that we could manufacture here in Melbourne. We printed a range of T shirts along with some stationery items. To ensure 'Guess What?' had a total point of difference, Alex and I made a follow-up trip to the USA and Japan.

Again we visited the gift fairs in LA, San Francisco, New York and Tokyo.

We collated orders with freight forwarders, allowing us to place modest orders with numerous suppliers.

Alex was skilled at sorting out any supply hiccups, as he didn't comprehend the word 'NO'.

We signed leases on shops in Carlton, South Yarra and Malvern after an extensive search. We papered the windows for the fit out period (one month) and only the pink neon sign reading 'Guess What?' was visible. We told no one what the shops were about, but I did ring in a number of talkback radio programs to get the rumour mill working. The plan of opening all three shops on the same day fell short by two days.

We just couldn't be in all three locations and control the crowds of teenagers that turned up.

In November 1983 we opened our first two shops in Carlton and South Yarra at midday. We had small queues of people eager to see what all the fuss was about.

Malvern opened two days later and attracted a much larger queue. We had to initiate the crowd control practice of 'two in-two out'. The private school girls went crazy over the baby's bottles packed with tiny jellybeans. We stayed back after hours to re-stock the shops. Guess What? was a huge success.

The Melbourne Sun newspaper (Friday 11/11/83) wrote,

"It seems hard to believe that anyone would open a shop selling merchandise that nobody needs".

Nobody needed a birthday card that looked like a legal summons or a complaint form that offered only a tiny writing pad, or doormat featuring your least favourite politician, either. But it worked. For me, the most satisfying aspect was that the giftware trade had no idea how we sourced product that it had never seen before. 'Point of difference'...that was the key. Guess What? gave us a huge adrenalin shot (that's a statement, not a question).

We opened a fourth shop in Camberwell some time later and we had many enquiries from other people who wanted to join the group. We didn't have the funds or expertise to franchise the concept and it was clear to me that

'Guess What?' had a limited lifecycle.

Before too long every Thomas, Richard and Harry climbed on the gravy train, and at the same time shop rents went through the roof. It took the copycats a while to catch up, but all too soon the market was totally overcrowded.

Our product sourcing trip to Japan, June 1983.

Centre is our buying agent, Harry San with Alex Bryla, David Glat, myself and two representatives from Kent Stationery, Tokyo.

Guess What?

Guess What? Malvern

Guess What? Carlton

22 - GO WEST YOUNG FAMILY

Change is good and a huge change is even 'gooder'!

I needed a new challenge. Kylie-Ann was coming up to high school age and I thought that Perth would be a much safer environment to bring up our children. Melbourne was becoming a tough city and I didn't like that. I wanted a fresh start. Also, I had run out of business ideas in Melbourne.

Yes, I know, it's all about me!

What do you expect from a eulogy, dear reader?

We had a friendship with the Elly family in Perth dating back to the 1970s. Clive and Glennys, who were pillars of the Baptist Church, ran a real estate business south of the river. Clive asked me if I'd be interested to come over and manage a business broking division he wanted to establish.

Helen and I flew over to Perth to discuss this opportunity, and we agreed to sell up in Blackburn and move west. It was a huge lifestyle change, especially for Helen, but she said she was on board. As it turned out, she wasn't totally and she swung like a pendulum for the next year or so. (I completely understand that, now.)

We travelled across to the west on the magnificent 'Indian Pacific' railway system. It was an amazing experience and I'd love to do it again, one day, but I've got a feeling that might not happen, for a number of reasons. The kids loved the compact sleeping arrangements and the dining car was an exciting highlight.

Helen wasn't exactly great company as I seem to remember. She had second thoughts on the whole move and certainly I took the brunt of her wrath at the time. It was an enormous life changing experience and whilst I was excited about what was to unfold, Helen was somewhat nervous. That's totally understandable and she came good...down the track (pun intended).

Lower property prices in Perth meant that we could buy very well there. Clive had a property in mind for us, one of his listings as it turned out. It was an impressive mock Tudor, two-storey, four-bedroom statement that shrieked 'look at me'.

The kids loved our new house in Booragoon, the mediterranean climate and the beautiful swimming pool.

In July '77, when I was 39 years old, I completed the course at the Real Estate Institute of WA to achieve my sales representative licence. The only information I took on board was to do with dispute resolution.

They taught the principle of 'feel, felt, found'.

"I know how you feel. I felt the same way too, but I found..." I've never used this crap, but I found...

So, now I had a 'commission only' career in real estate. The open-plan office offered no privacy and everyone's phone conversations were shared by all. The staff turnover, even for the short time I was involved, was sky high.

The business broking division hadn't eventuated; consequently, I was in the residential property sales office with a discombobulated group of mismatched hopefuls. One, very attractive female rep seemed to have a very special relationship with the principal. She was married with a young family, whilst he, our esteemed leader, was an elder in the Baptist church. Nothing to see here! Move on.

Most of the hopeful, enthusiastic sales representatives, the ones that stayed on, were falling well short of making a satisfactory living. Like most other real estate companies, CEJ continued to run sales meetings and seminars to rev up and keep the 'team' onside. (Going forward) Real Estate jargon is cliche' rich.

One such team-building, motivational program that stayed in my memory was titled 'Towards Excellence'.

Clive had commissioned an external marketing guru to lift the 'team'. The 'Towards Excellence' twentypage, spiral bound manual that was handed out at the end of the seminar had one page upside down.

'Towards Mediocrity' may have been a more suitable seminar title.

My limited experience inside this industry confirmed that I wanted no part in it.

Our dear leader was clearly playing around, and I'm not talking golf.

Mike Kaufman had joined the company a few months before I arrived. He was a mechanical engineer looking for a retirement income. He was a very clever, funny, English gentleman and I really enjoyed his company.

We discussed the comings and goings in the office. The hypocritical behaviour of our leader appalled Mike. We both knew that we needed to escape this dysfunctional circus. I managed to achieve a couple of small sales commissions before listing a quite interesting little business. Mike and I got together to discuss the possibilities. It was a very small recycling collection round, with huge potential; or so we thought. We purchased that business together and it was goodbye to the real estate industry.

The business we purchased was pretty basic. It used a ten-tonne tray truck, with two bins for the collection of empty wine bottles and aluminium cans. It had set collection rounds, which included major hotels and the casino complex.

We changed the business name to 'Container Recycling' and smartened up the collection arrangements. It was a six-day collection cycle, so two days a week we worked solo, otherwise together.

One memorable pickup I was making in St Georges Terrace, comes to mind. I drove the truck into the very tight CBD pickup spot in the underground carpark, blocking the exit lane for one minute.

A guy in a massive Mercedes Benz went berserk. I said, "Sorry mate, I'll only be a minute". He screamed, "

Do you know who I am"? "No idea", I replied. He said "I'm Alan Bond and I have a doctor's appointment". I added, "I'm not surprised". He didn't recognise me, either. So he said!

The collected bottles were taken to a recycling yard in the inner eastern suburbs. It was heavy, dirty work, but not at all taxing on the brain. We had planned to expand the business and hire others to do the heavy lifting, but the recycling centre went into receivership four months after we purchased the business. It had been owned by a group of disgraced businessmen associated with the infamous WA Inc scandal. We were owed a considerable amount of money, but these guys played by their own rules.

We made other arrangements for the purchase of our recyclable loads, but took a substantial drop in load prices. The potential to grow the business was now dubious at best. 'Container Recycling' was not able to support two families, so we sold out. Mike went back to engineering and I went back to the drawing board.

In the days before the invention of the 'drawing board', I wonder what people went back to.

Our new home in Booragoon

First day at a new school

My little Savage Tasman at Rottnest Island. Sometimes the return voyage became a tiny bit willing. It can get quite rough when the sea breeze strengthens.

23 - SHOWBITS

Perth offered a very pleasant lifestyle and our family settled in to enjoy the moderate Mediterranean climate, the clean air and uncluttered roads. The white sand beaches were unsurpassed, and I bought a little half cabin cruiser to explore the waterways. It was a fifteen-foot Savage Tasman with a 50- horsepower outboard motor. It cost me $7,250, and I just loved it!

Perth is the furthest capital city from any other capital city in the world. In the nineties you could feel this, especially when you needed some obscure part for the car or a rare CD. "We'll get it from the Eastern States" was the catch phrase. The retail shops in my field of interest were way behind those on the other side of the Nullarbor.

No one had mastered the 'Guess What' concept in the West. I knew the formula backwards and I knew where mistakes were made. I had the contacts in the East and overseas so it was a no-brainer to go again, but this time I would have a showbiz theme and I would go solo. No partners. I registered the business name 'Showbits'. (Showbiz and Shoebiz were taken by a footwear retailer)

I planned the product mix, which I had fine tuned somewhat over the years. I had close friends in the industry and I visited the Sydney and Melbourne gift fairs to catch up and tick all the boxes.

I was able to source some product from Perth wholesalers but a small number of local suppliers gave me the unwelcome treatment. 'We don't need Eastern Staters coming over here, thanks'; especially when I mentioned that I was opening in Perth CBD.

The most welcoming and useful local supplier was Skansen Giftware, owned and operated by Manny Stul, who today is a billionaire and the CEO of Moose Toys. In the mid eighties Skansen had a modest office/ warehouse in the Perth inner suburb of Subiaco. Manny did everything himself: sales, invoicing and packing. Skansen became a huge publicly listed, giftware wholesaler and publisher of the famous 'Elle' calendars, and one of my major suppliers for a long time.

I negotiated a lease in the Carillon Arcade, right smack bang in the city centre. Prior to the shop opening, there was no room for cars in the double garage at home. It was full of stock.

One local wholesaler said he couldn't supply me a particular stationery range, as another retailer had pressured him not to supply. No problem, I'll simply make arrangements with my east coast mates.

Showbits wasn't as whimsical as Guess What? Initially, I concentrated on movie star merchandise plus I stocked a unique range of American and Japanese confectionery that had never been seen in Perth stores.

American sporting trading cards became all the rage, particularly NBA (basketball) and American league football cards. Not only did we run the cards, but also as much associated merchandise as I could get my hands on, including T-shirts, shorts and caps. I asked my staff to wear the gear. They loved getting free uniforms!

I was regularly importing trading cards and accessories by airfreight from my supplier in San Francisco.

In year three, we moved across the aisle in the shopping centre to a much a bigger store. I fitted out the new, much bigger shop like a TV studio, to add to retail experience. It's all about selling the sizzle, not the sausage. Billy Graham knew all about that!

I knew how to attract publicity to my retail stores. I had mastered the art at Kinderplay and Guess What?

When the first Elle McPherson calendars were released (by Skansen Giftware) I had a life-size cardboard cutout of the supermodel, and a huge poster of her in the window that had the hand-written message...

'Thanks for a great night John, love Elle'.

My young client base could not believe how lucky I'd been. They didn't twig to the fact that, maybe, someone else wrote that note!

We had a very sophisticated shrink-wrapping machine in the warehouse. In the early nineties I sold sealed, autographed Elvis calendars, despite the fact that he had left the building in 1977.

In 1992 the Reserve Bank released the first polymer $5 banknote in Australia. I pre-ordered 500 notes. On the note's release date I advertised the new $5 notes at $4.95 each (limit one per purchase).

I rang every TV station in Perth and advised the news departments that some idiot was selling $5 notes fo $4.95 in Perth city. Thank you Channel 7.

Showbits stocked an extensive range of movie star postcards and fairly bad taste greeting cards. All pretty harmless but some people took exception to a few particular titles. The nativity scene with the Jesus declaring "it's a girl" offended a few. One drab, cardigan-wearing fellow spent about an hour going through our range until he found one that offended him. He made a huge song and dance about how disgusting one particular title was. I simply said, "That took you an hour to find, next time, just ask for assistance".

One of my American suppliers suggested I get onto the 'Simpsons' merchandise. He sent me a series of oversize Simpsons' postcards. They sold like hot cakes! I'd not heard of Bart Simpson and his dysfunctional family, but this range was hot.

I worked with a very good local T-shirt screen printer and he was able to scan the postcards, make the screens and supply me with the first Simpsons' T-shirts in the West.

Some months later a guy came into the shop and told me his company had exclusive rights to this franchise. He asked me to withdraw from sale all Simpsons merchandise. I asked him for proof of his claim. We had a classic standoff. I'd had experience with this emerging conflict and wasn't too concerned.

A few letters and demands were made, but soon enough the next big character merchandise arrived and we moved on. The goal was to be one step ahead. The girls who worked for me, including my daughters, seemed to have a keen 'range radar'.

I had some wonderful young ladies working for me over the years, and I'm still in touch with quite a few. I send a big shout out to Sophie, Shazza, Squirt and Kalika Duck, and all the terrific, switched on team.

Yo-Yos were go!

I got a tipoff from Chris Noel at The Novelty Warehouse in Sydney that yo-yos were making a big time comeback. He was supplying a basic model for a couple of dollars wholesale and he let drop that Sydney retailers were selling huge quantities and he could hardly keep up with demand. I jumped on board. I was also getting feedback that Japan was producing a high quality, beautifully balanced range of hi-tech yoyos.

A few phone calls later I tracked down the importer to a one-man business in Melbourne. This guy had supplied a few items to Kinderplay in earlier days. We had a good business relationship and as stock of the Japanese-made yo-yos was limited I'd get first option for Western Australia.

The 'Brain' yo-yo had a built in clutch mechanism that made performing tricks much easier. We retailed these at $19.95 and we sold many thousand units every month for the next ten months. They also manufactured professional models selling at $69 and $125.

I ran a number of Yo-Yo competitions in Forest Place (central Perth) and produced a small booklet featuring the best 35 tricks as demonstrated by our young customers. I supplied the books to a number of other retailers in the East.

One hot February afternoon I came home to find a guy wrecking the kids' bathroom in our Booragoon house. He seemed like a nice enough fellow, but I asked for an explanation. (That's only fair, I thought.)

He explained that Helen had engaged him to remodel the kids' bathroom, as he was a tiler after all. Helen must have forgotten to let me know about this little renovation. This mystery tiler explained that his (then) wife worked with Helen, and that's how it came to this. I asked him if he'd like some water before I headed off.

"Where are you going?" he enquired. I told him that I was about to drop the boat in the river for a little sunset fishing.

"Great", he said, " 'mind if I come too?" I didn't even know his name! It was Graham...and still is.

I like to refer to Graham as a white collar tiler. While other tradies may like a battered sausage and a coke for lunch, Graham might choose a smoked salmon bagel with capers and a fresh, lightly chilled cranberry juice served in a nicely balanced glass.

We've been great mates ever since this unlikely meeting although I'm still paying off the renovation, in kind.

I had a large warehouse in the shopping centre tower and I shared the space with freelance giftware agent, Graeme Hynes. He was a smart young guy who knew how to run with an idea. He started making oversized crazy hats in AFL (Australian Football League) club colours. He was having them made up in Bali and they were selling well, Australia wide. Soon the 'cease and desist' demands started arriving from lawyers acting for the AFL and Graeme was completely spooked out. I called my solicitor (Richard's brother) Ken Opat. He'd guided me out of numerous similar close scrapes over many years. His advice to me was "tell your mate to apologise and apply for the licence". He did and it was on a winner. Graeme also manufactured a number of 'slogan' items, such as stubby holders, coffee cups and bumper stickers. He agreed to work with me at Showbits and I would reciprocate.

Writing crazy slogans was right up my alley. They say 'plagiarising' is copying from one source, research is compiling from numerous sources.

'Which Bank? They're All Bastards'. That's one of mine!

So is 'Astrology is Taurus'.

We printed a blank-paged book titled 'The Wit and Wisdom of Pauline Hanson'. That would still sell today.

Showbits was really rocketing along and I soon had people wanting to open their own store under the banner. Again, I didn't have the funds or the expertise to franchise the business, and like Guess What? back in Melbourne I opted for a licence model. I would allow a licensee to use the name and brand for a once-off fee and an ongoing small commission. I would assist in finding the sites, shop fitting, establishing the supply lines and the general operational matters. I would supply a small range of items such as yo-yos.

For a few years this went very well. We grew to ten Showbits stores with varying degrees of success. A few stores changed hands and some operators were not successful. Rents and interest rates were skyrocketing and trading conditions were becoming very difficult indeed. Copycat stores were thinning out the takings.

Whilst all this was happening Helen and I were drifting apart.

I felt I was living in a vacuum.

It was so painful to see life taking such an unplanned and unwelcome course. I moved out of the family home to a two-bedroom apartment nearby. Ky was doing her thing and rarely home, Katie was at university and wasn't so happy at home. Emily was engrossed in her final year of secondary school, sport being her stand-out area. She was a very keen water polo player and made it into the state under-16 team. I was working long hours between Showbits and Graeme's projects when Skansen offered him a senior position in sales and product development. Skansen was now Australia's leading company in its field.

The general manager was Tony Gilding, who was totally 'switched on' in the giftware industry. Tony was the first person I ever met who used the new communication system, email. It was slow and clunky and could never catch on.

Tony and Manny asked me to join the company for a buying trip to the US.

My Skansen business card read 'Vice President, Marketing'.

My Showbits card listed my qualifications as Q.C. (Qantas Club)

L.B.C. (Lego Building Certificate) and S.S.C. (Senior Swimming Certificate)

Skansen had its own registered travel division which attracted industry rates and upgrades. These guys were smart, and when we stayed in New York, we had the best rates for first-class otel accommodation. I really enjoyed my short time with Skansen, but I had family matters at home that were spiralling out of control and I had to concentrate on extinguishing or, at least, controlling the bushfires.

I remember sitting in my 6th floor office/warehouse thinking,
'OK, what's the worst case scenario'?
Scary thoughts passed my mind.

Showbits wasn't meeting its running costs and I had a lease to see out. Overdraft interest rates hit 19%.

The management at the Carillon Arcade in Perth CBD was totally unsympathetic to the situation and managed by faceless beancounters. Most, if not all, traders were experiencing disastrous trading times. I was confronted with a downhill spiral on many fronts. Difficult times, indeed.

I had an offer from a Melbourne based wholesale gift company to become their buyer. This would mean a good deal of overseas travel, read 'running away'. Katie was managing the shop and doing a great job under extremely trying circumstances. She was so strong in so many ways.

I ran away.

I took the giftware buyer position and visited the world's greatest toy and gift fairs buying for someone else with their money. It was exciting and lonely at the same time, plus I felt guilty leaving two sinking ships.

My colleague, Graeme Hynes, was now also working for the same company at this stage. I liked working on projects again with this smart young guy.

After a few months as buyer, I was made Australian sales manager of this giftware wholesaler. I didn't want this role, but it was 'take it or leave'. I couldn't afford the latter.

The principal of this company clearly had a serious anger management problem. He paid good money, but for this he 'owned' his staff.

He chewed up and spat out so many good people. Most re-grouped but one woman in accounts had a terrible breakdown due to his constant bullying behaviour. It became a truly horrible work environment.

That's why I haven't named this company.

I could see the writing clearly on the wall. Showbits had to be wound up. I had to take the fall to protect Helen. I contacted all my suppliers and made payment arrangements as best I could. Most were understanding of the situation, and bent over backwards to take back stock and agree to a nominal final payment. One major Perth supplier (AI), who enjoyed sales of an estimated $7.5 million from the combined Showbits group, refused to co-operate, and even had a go at Helen, who had no day-to-day dealings in the business.

"We were talking pennies, Geoff, compared with the business we brought your way".

Here's another little fact.

The other un-named company (CM) that I worked for in Melbourne used this Perth wholesaler (AI) as its exclusive WA agent. Melbourne (CM) supplied Perth (AI) with its exclusive trading card and accessory range while Perth company (AI) was back dooring the same items from a supplier in the US.

Melbourne company (CM) was supplying two other exclusive distributors in WA at this time. Both parties were cheating on each other, big time.

I failed to come to a satisfactory settlement agreement with these guys.

Showbits was no more and neither was the marriage of Helen and John.

We distributed thousands of free passes to allow people to visit Showbits and spend a few dollars. Those without a free pass were also permitted to spend up!

We custom-printed these booklets for a number of retailers across Australia. They sold for $1 and we asked kids to send illustrations of their own tricks for publication in the next print run. The successful kids won a 'Brain' yo yo. Hundreds of hand drawn little tricks had to be tested by own panel and re-drawn by our own graphic artist.

Thanks to my friend, Tony Carlin, of Logical Choice for this pic.

Showbits Carillon Arcade store in Perth

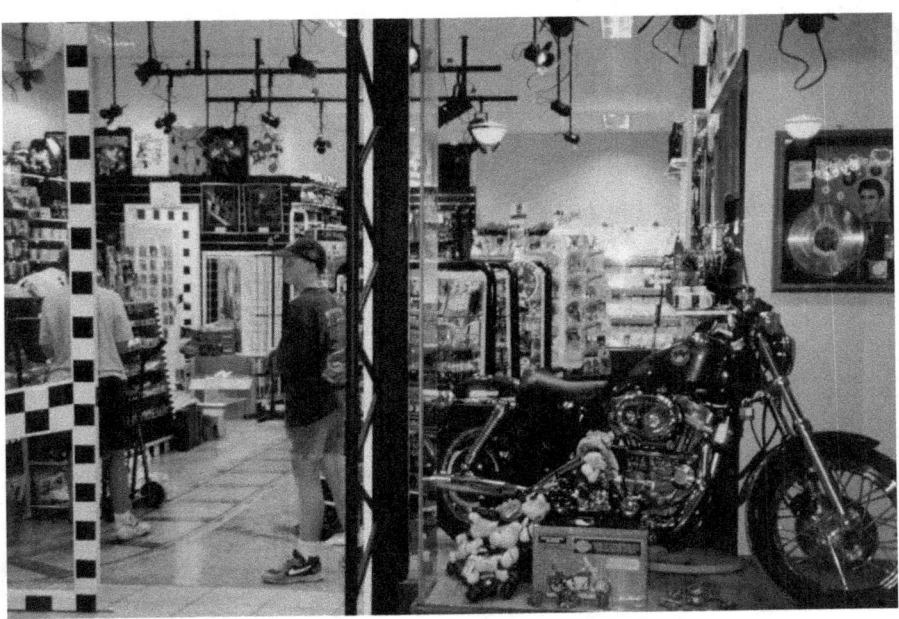

24 - NEWMARKET MUSIC

While I was still working for that toxic company, I had moved back from Perth to Melbourne to live. Graeme suggested we rent a flat together but I needed my own space. He looked around Hawthorn but I wanted to be closer to my friends around Elsternwick. I leased a newly renovated two bedroom unit in Elwood. I was also looking to move on from the giftware trade. I began re-connecting with my muso contacts. The Melbourne jazz scene was still bouncing along with a number of popular venues attracting good, enthusiastic audiences. Richard was playing in a couple of pretty darn good groups and I was keen to tag along. I was single and not so interested in much outside work and music. I did have a date with a much younger woman, which was set up by a friend, but this failed at the first hurdle.

My group of friends would go to various jazz sessions and it was through this group that I met Lynn. We had sort of known each other from Richard's time playing with New Harlem and later, The Creole Bells. I had no idea that she lived in Elwood, eight minutes walk from my flat. After a few more chance meetings, I invited her for dinner at my place, but as I wasn't a smooth operator I invited another six people as a safety net.

I cheated. I bought prepared food and pretended to serve it direct from my little kitchen. Lynn spotted that the oven had never been used and I had to admit to my shameful deceit!

It was a very strange, unsophisticated dinner party but we all enjoyed the takeaways and a few laughs.

Some time later Lynn invited me to a grape grazing session in the Yarra Valley. That went better and slowly, very slowly, we hooked up.

My time with CM was coming to a most welcome end.

I approached Greg and Daniel at Dex Audio to discuss working with them. They now had a serious recording studio and distribution division, Newmarket Music. I suggested that I come on board and set up a children's division. I still had my contacts with a number of artists and suppliers that I had at Kinderplay, so I could offer a fine catalogue of children's CDs and compact cassettes.

We negotiated a deal and I was back in the music business.

Happy days again! These guys treated me with unqualified respect and I gave them my best. Lynn and I decided to head off by train to the Mittagong Jazz Festival in the Southern Highlands, just south of Sydney. The venue was a private girls college. We both knew many of the musicians and patrons. It was a three day festival with dozens of guests staying in the girls' boarding house, whilst the school girls were on holidays. It was a hoot!

The program featured the very best jazz talent Australia had to offer. It was a feast for the ears. I had two working ears in those days! One absolute standout performance was by The String Band.

George Washingmachine (violin) and Ian Date (guitar) in concert with Stan Valacos (bass) and John and David Blenkhorn also on guitars. Their venue was a lecture theatre with stepped, single desks facing a blackboard. George held the audience in the palm of his hand with his headmaster-like routine. The band was precise in its delivery.

After the show I approached George (aka Stephen Washington) to discuss recording The String Band with Newmarket Music. I had no authority to do so, but I just knew the project would work.

Greg took me at my word and Newmarket Music funded the recording. We flew the band to Melbourne for a three-day recording session.

Buying an airline ticket for a bloke known as 'George Washingmachine' caused an interesting reaction from the Qantas staff, but these were the days before the strict security procedures. Ian Date was such a character in his own right. When we were discussing the title for this recording, he suggested 'A Dingo Has Taken My Baby'. I preferred 'The String Band'.

Our audio engineer at Newmarket Studios was the very talented Ben Hurt. He was a pleasure to work with and the recording sessions were textbook perfect. Musicians always gained extra confidence when Ben was at the forty-channel mixing desk. After the first take of the first the session, we all knew we had a very worthwhile project in the making. Everyone knew their role in the production and it all went swimmingly.

The album was released in August 2001 and is still listed in the Newmarket Music catalogue.

Newmarket Music was managed by PBSFM jazz presenter, Gerry Koster. He had an extensive knowledge of contemporary jazz, but little interest in my preferred styles. That made for a good mix. I was only working a four-day week at the office. If I had a recording project in mind, I would submit a budget and marketing plan to the directors and, usually, get on with it. I made a number of projects with George and then teamed him up with the absolutely wonderful Julie O'Hara. Their first album together was such a joy to work on, in every way possible. The chemistry worked and still does today. The first album, 'Paper Moon', was followed up with 'Midnight Sun'. Julie and George often perform together and I always love catching up with these sublime musicians.

Gerry moved on and I was promoted to the big chair at Newmarket Music. I worked on many recordings and releases over the next few years. We had a substantial stable of very talented local recording artists and bands and our label went from strength to strength. I acquired the services of Paris Wells to help run Newmarket. I explained to Paris that she was my assistant. She insisted she was the assistant manager, but I suggested that she was 'assistant to the manager'. She signed off as ATTM. I loved working with Paris and she went on to enjoy a good deal of fame as a pop singer/songwriter. Paris toured widely with Justin Timberlake. Apparently, that's impressive!

At Newmarket Music we slowed down on imports and concentrated on albums that would be recorded at our studios resulting in CD mastering, artwork and manufacturing in house, by Dex Audio. It made sense.

Dex Audio had Australia's most efficient CD manufacturing plant. We could also boast that we had one of the finest mastering engineers, Adam Dempsey, and an amazing art studio headed by Jamie Coghill. My goal was to increase in-house production. Why wouldn't we support our own incredible crew? And we did and it worked.

I copped an uncomfortable serve of agro from some jazz radio presenters who had for years enjoyed being sampled with unique overseas product that resulted in few sales. Being a fairly 'commercial animal', I understood that this activity, while it gave the label some industry cred, was costing the label money it didn't have. It had to stop. One of Lucky Ocean's producers at ABC Radio National wasn't happy. He was on that gravy train for many a year. Boy, did he give me a serve; Ouch!

Streaming was on the horizon and we reluctantly signed up with Apple Music. This resulted in fewer CD sales, less in-house activity and lower royalties to our artists. It wasn't something I wanted to be involved with, but the hype sucked in so many musicians. They wanted to be listed on the streaming giants' list. The only winner was Apple.

I'm not convinced that all our recording artists realised or totally understood that CDs were supplied to retailers on a sale or return basis. If the artist/band didn't attract sales, the product came back to us. No sale, no royalty.

I do remember one very angry call from a well known artist who gave me a mega-serve about her album not being displayed at JB Hi Fi. I checked the details and we had delivered stock to all aforementioned stores. After the obligatory period, set by the stores, 95% of stock was returned. I didn't need that unfair treatment at the time but I understand her frustration. She continues to be a fine performer on the Australian jazz scene to this day, and I wish her well.

It's tough out there!

Record stores were closing right, left and centre across Australia. CD sales dived. That's progress...is it?

Another New Start

Hooking up with Lynn had given me a whole new lease on life. She had been in a long term relationship that fell apart, and the timing for us both seemed right. I was clearly the winner as Lynn is a people magnet. She attracts interesting, warm people and has strong family values. Her extended family and friends made me feel very welcome and comfortable.

Lynn and I married in 2004 and what a party we had at Lynn's brother and sister-in-law's home, in Glen Waverley. I referred to the ceremony as a meeting of John the Baptist and Moses. Lynn and I wrote the very liberal order of service, the celebrant did his legally required oration and the party began.

George Washingmachine, Miles White and Howard Cairns made up the official trio and a few of our guests, including Ian Smith and the best man, Richard, brought their instruments. The night rocked along.

Lynn's mother, Ilse and her sister, Ellen, danced like they hadn't in decades. It was a very happy event.

Lynn's wedding dress was fashioned from a bedspread as that was the fabric she chose; plus as a bonus, it came with two matching cushions. Peter and Helen were wonderful hosts and the catering was first class.

Baby Classics

Everything was going along quite nicely at Newmarket Music and I decided to make a few video programs for children in my spare time. I'd acquired a copy of an American program 'Baby Mozart' on VHS tape. This was a huge success, world wide. I thought, "I could do that".

There were a number of similar programs to Baby Mozart on the market in Europe, and I managed to get copies of a few of these. I studied the content and set about planning my first Baby Classics video. I was quite experienced with video production, but I needed the music score. I called Allan Zavod and he came over to discuss what I had in mind. He was classically trained and had moved back to Melbourne, but he could not commit to working on such a project as he was in such demand on all fronts. We also discussed making a jazz album for Newmarket Music but his budget requirements were way out of our league. Allan had suggested that James Morrison play on a couple of tracks but his suggested fee was greater than the total budget, times two or three. As always, it was nice to catch up, though.

I tried a few other bods without success, then I managed to connect with Stephen Paix. This brilliant young musician was a perfect fit. He was always hungry so Lynn would feed him up while I motivated him to join my project. The first thing was to record an album for the Newmarket children's catalogue, titled 'Twinkle, Twinkle Little Mozart'.

I could get a budget for this and the CD was commercially successful. Now, I had my copyright-free score to use on the first video.

The next step was to film cute and interesting images to edit to the music. This took me about one year to finalise, as I also had a fair workload with Newmarket Music at the time.

Together with Steve providing the score, I made three Baby Classics titles which were first released on VHS tapes. Later these went to DVD, but marketing was challenging as I didn't have the funds to capitalise the launch of this range. I only had a few toy shops and kindergarten suppliers, including Kinderplay, selling these programs plus my own website.

Two years later I got a call from Hinkler Books. The CEO's little kids loved my videos and he wanted to rebrand the programs, add a series of related books, and release them world wide. His advertising gurus planned to reposition (that's guru speak) these under the name 'Weeny Boppers'.

(What the F!#* was wrong with 'Baby Classics?')

They spent serious money and much time on the new packaging before discovering that the word 'Weeny' in some cultures refers to a sausage and is a euphemism for 'penis.' Back to the drawing board and another expensive delay. They rebranded as 'Baby Boppers'. Wrong again. Bop can mean to 'hit' in English-speaking countries.

The packaging was pretty good and if they had stuck with the original 'Baby Classics' name; well, who knows?

So much for the advertising/marketing gurus.

From time to time Stephen Washington (aka George Washingmachine) would stay overnight with us when he had a gig in Melbourne. On a few occasions he brought his Mum, Sadie Bishop, over for afternoon tea.

Lynn loved to put on a special spread and Sadie, George's famous, guitar virtuoso mother, would entertain us in the kitchen, with Lynn's old guitar. She was one of Australia's leading classical guitarists and teachers: such a delightful lady.

Newmarket Music had its challenges with all the changes in how music was being delivered, but it was so rewarding to be involved with recording sessions with so many great singers and musicians.

Many other artists came to us with their finished recordings. As online streaming was becoming more popular, physical CD sales were plummeting. CDs were supplied to retailers on a sale-or-return basis. It became a huge problem for artists who didn't have a high profile, and more were beginning to give me a very hard time when their titles were not successful at the retail level.

Here's a list of those difficult individuals. No. I don't think I should go there!

Hearing Loss

I went to a Friday night football game at Docklands with a group of guys from Perth. During the match the fellow sitting on my left put two fingers in his mouth and let out an incredibly loud whistle. He repeated this until I insisted he stop. I moved away.

Next morning I still had a ringing in my ears. My phone rang while I was having a coffee with Richard. No one there. It rang again; again no one…Richard said he could hear that someone was on the other end.

I changed ears and on my starboard side I could hear. Port side, nothing. I did have a cold so I thought I might be blocked up a bit.

I rang my GP. He said "get down here, now". He did some simple hearing tests and sent me off to the Eye and Ear Hospital where I had a thorough hearing assessment. They put me on a course of steroids and made follow-up appointments, including a very scary MRI at Peter MacCallum Cancer Centre. The results suggested nerve deafness.

My left ear was never to recover and my right ear had cochlea hair damage. The hospital suggested I attended a speech (lip) reading course just in case my remaining hearing deteriorated further.

As we get our sense of direction from stereo hearing, one ear doesn't facilitate this rather useful function.

So now I'm running a music recording and distribution business with half an ear. The guys at work were all terrific and very understanding. Daniel, at Dex Audio, did say that he'd rather be blind than deaf. I pointed out that I wasn't offered a choice, at the time.

I outsourced the listening functions to Ben Hurt and Adam Dempsey, but when musicians wanted to come in and discuss new projects it became unworkable. I couldn't listen to demo recordings with the artist and go through the required steps to seeing a project home. I was living with the threat of further hearing loss.

"Pardon, say again, what was that?" Before I resigned I made a sign for the noticeboard in the tearoom at Dex Audio, advertising a set of left-sided speakers. My days at Newmarket Music were over.

As a footnote (ear-note)

I now have hi-tech hearing aids. The left side is a mic that transmits to the right side hearing aid which performs all the amplification tricks. I hear from both sides in my right ear only.

Speak to me on the left and I may look right!

My virtually undetectable hearing device

The String Band

George Washingmachine & Ian Date recording with John Blenkhorn, David Blenkhorn and Stan Valacos at Newmarket studios in North Melbourne, June 2001. Recording engineer Ben Hurt is at the 40-channel mixing deck, once owned by Neil Young.

The recording session of Allan Browne's Australian Jazz Band: 'Five Bells and Other Inspirations' featuring:
John Scurry,
Howard Cairns
Jo Stephenson
Eugene Ball
Steve Grant

25 - WAY BEYOND MELBOURNE

Lynn introduced me to her wonderful Swiss friends, Nils and Senta, who live in a quaint little village, outside Zurich. I'm not permitted to use the word 'village', as Brugg was declared a city more than a hundred years ago. But it does look like a village. Sorry.

In 2007 we returned to Switzerland and I took some video of their son, Mattis, going off to pre-school in the forest. Lynn and I had never seen anything like this. The preschoolers were at kinder in the wild! This was a weekly event before the winter set in. It made amazing footage. Matt's sister, Liv, who was about seven, added to the visuals with her make-believe play in the forest.

Back in Australia, Katie was teaching at a remote primary school outside Fitzroy Crossing, in the West Australian Kimberley region. I couldn't help thinking about the enormous contrast and mentioned the forest pre-school footage to Katie. She said her indigenous school children would love to see it, and they'd also be amazed to see how kids live in a big city. I'm certain that the vice is versa!

I set about filming kids getting to school on trams and trains, going up escalators, riding scooters, playing on the beach…just being kids in a big city.

I edited the footage and in June 2008 we headed North West, via Broome. Melbourne's winter is bleak but up there it's the dry season. We flew to Broome, rented a car and four hours later we were at the famous Fitzroy Crossing.

The town wasn't so safe to walk around after dark due to packs of threatening looking dogs that roamed the streets. They tended to be 'community dogs' rather than family pets. They're fine for the locals but not so with intruders.

Accommodation options were very limited. This town is a transit stop for the vast number of road trains and 'Grey Nomads' travelling in the North West. The latter take their homes with them.

We didn't feel that we were particularly suited to caravanning! I had experienced it in a former life as a much younger man but I couldn't see Lynn and me in such a confined space, travelling for weeks and weeks, without a deli in sight.

So, Dear Reader, we opted for 'Glamping' (glamour camping).

Our camp was set up on a cement slab with a fair sized tent that featured a fibreglass wet room; a little pod with a toilet and shower. The little green tree frogs loved our humid pod and every creepy crawly in town would visit if one crumb of food was on offer.

The camp stretcher beds were designed to enforce minimum sleep cycles. Best to go to bed late and get up early.

By 8 am you could have cooked an egg on the side of our tent. Abundant wildlife made this an interesting place to spend a night or two, but we were there for a week. The road out of town looked pretty good. Katie's school was off that road, on the 2.5 million-acre Gogo Cattle Station. The school was well equipped with the classrooms each having a number of air-conditioning units. The children were drawn from half a dozen communities, and bussed in and out each school day. I obtained permission to travel on one of these buses. I wasn't authorised to film in the communities, but I did get some great footage of these happy, noisy, enthusiastic kids heading off for the day's activities. They had so much fun on the bus with this white guy and his video camera.

Many of the 120 kids had suffered some hearing loss due to untreated infections and consequently the teachers needed to use amplification equipment.

The days heated up very early so outdoor activities commenced well before classes. Many of these kids are very good little athletes. The skills they displayed on the sports ground amazed us.

Watching the barefoot kids playing football on a dusty, dry pitch was a real eyeopener. One little girl sat next to me, not watching the game, just staring at me. She couldn't hold it in any longer.

She just blurted out, "What's that mister"? She was pointing to my second chin.

No one had ever asked me that question. Her eyes were fixed, wide open on me and my generous, jowly, upper front neckline. I explained that we're all different and this is how I'm built.

Thankfully, the school bell rang and she ran off to class.

The kids were bilingual, at the least. When they called to each other in the playground, I couldn't understand a word.

Katie had an assistant teacher who spoke Kreole; the local dialect.

Showtime

It was time to show the video.

Katie set up a big screen TV in the classroom and I set up a camera to film the kids' reactions. It was a circus! They just loved seeing their counterparts riding on trams and trains and doing things they could never imagine. The escalator scenes were a huge hit and brought shrieks of laughter. "How the hell do they do that?" one kid yelled. It was so funny; we were all crying tears of laughter. Other classes heard the carry-on and we had many repeat screenings.

I showed them the footage of themselves watching the screen. It was all just too funny.

26 - THE LADY AT THE MARKET

We met a Lao lady at a Sunday morning market who was the sister of a friend of Lynn's mum (stay with me). She asked us what we planned for the holiday period and mentioned that she and her husband had a guest house in Luang Prabang, Laos, with plenty of rooms available at ridiculously cheap rates. I asked if I could get access to filming school kids there to add to my film project. 'Can do' was the response.

The following January we flew to Luang Prabang, via Bangkok, having had no idea what to expect.

It was like turning the clock back fifty years, with the UNESCO-protected city buzzing with motor bikes and tuk-tuks and pleasingly few private cars.

Their villa was a fair walk into the main street and our hosts used little golf carts to get about. The accommodation was pretty basic yet clean and comfortable. There was a very cold swimming pool and a covered outdoor kitchen with shared dining tables. The town centre is near to the confluence of the Mekong and Khan rivers. Despite its broken infrastructure, power outages and wonky little bamboo bridges, we just loved this little jewel on the Mekong. We still do, although as the years roll on it's becoming more and more touristy and the Chinese influence is changing the landscape, not necessarily for the better.

Our hosts are Lao people who live in Melbourne and spend a few months in Luang Prabang each year.

Our school filming visit was cleared with the authorities, but at the last minute just as we boarded the golf cart, our hosts, Phay and Tou, let drop that the school was in fact an orphanage school. The six hundred children who attend school also live there on the outskirts of town, well out of sight.

As we turned into the pot-holed unmade road that took us to the school, there were kids everywhere. We were met by a couple of teachers who led us to the ramshackle class rooms at the end of the quadrangle.

The desks were only just holding together and the blackboards were barely readable. The conditions were appalling by our standards but the teachers and students knew no other.

The kids loved being filmed and crowded around me for a sneak preview of the footage. A few kids had a smattering of English but weren't conversational. Tou and Phay translated for us.

Just as I completed the classroom footage an almighty 'CLANG' rang out.

A truck wheel rim hanging from a low hanging tree branch was being whacked with a length of pipe. It was lunch time!

The steaming room had been busy with its huge rice-filled buckets cooking over open fires. The kids on cooking duties were preparing the sticky rice which was shovelled (literally) into sacks and taken to the tables in the food hall. The kids brought their own individual bowls to their allocated table. It was standing room only...no space for seating in the food hall. I filmed as the kids were served by their fellow students.

The younger kids, say seven and eight-year olds, were helped by the older kids. There was no sign of greed or anger.

I had to steel myself for this unbelievable situation.

Kids feeding kids with sticky rice and a soupy vegetable supplement. I turned to see Phay crying his eyes out. He later told me he had no idea what was happening with his people, but this was reality and is to this day in many parts of the undeveloped world.

When the kids' bowls were full they headed off to enjoy their meal with their mates. The girls mostly went back to their dormitories while many of the boys found somewhere to dine, outside.

They all held over a portion of sticky rice for their evening meal as the food hall was only open at lunchtime.

The orphanage school had girls' dorms to the left, boys to the right. Each side had a toilet block (squat... no paper) and a bath area. They bathe outside the large communal bath. The girls wash clothed, for modesty. They also wash their clothing at the same time. Many had only two or three sets of clothing and many kids did not have a towel. The water was not heated and it does get very cold in winter. The toilets were disgusting in every way possible.

The younger children slept on low wooden benches with thin individual mats, about twenty-five children in each row. The older kids had bunk beds packed in close together to sleep as many kids as possible per dorm.

The kids knew of no other lifestyle and made the best of every situation. They made up their own games and the playgrounds were full of kids running, laughing and playing ball with whatever they could find.

There appeared to be very little, if any, sexual attraction between the girls and the boys, even though the leaving age was 19 years.

After lunch we were introduced to a sixteen-year-old student who ran the art room. Seng Song had been here since he was eight years old. He was an enormously talented artist who made it his business to study English and art in every free moment. The art room was severely under resourced, but the works by the students were offered for sale to visitors, and this facilitated replacement art materials and improvements.

We purchased a couple of watercolour paintings by Seng Song and treasure these to this day.

The first day at the orphanage school saw us all emotionally drained. That evening we sat down around the dining table to discuss how we could make the kids' lives a little bit easier. Firstly, we needed funds. I sent an email to everyone on my contact list explaining the situation. I asked for a $50 donation which we would match, to buy essentials for the kids. The response was fantastic, although I did tread on a few toes.

A few said 'NO'. That's OK. One person suggested that we were giving the kids false hopes.

Can you believe that, dear reader?

Within four days we had $2350 which we matched. Our first goal was to give every child (and every teacher) a bath towel, a toothbrush and toothpaste.

Tou and Phay had the contacts at the local Pousi market and arranged bulk buy prices. We paid $1.80ea on our order of 630 towels but could only get these in 8 different colour ranges, so on distribution we had permanent ink pens and little sewing kits on hand for the kids to distinguish their own towel.

We had to hire two large tuk-tuks to pick up and deliver the goods. On the same day we gave out pens, books, shampoo and soap plus a dozen soccer balls and basketballs to share.

We raked in a few helpers for the big distribution event. Lynn's family friend, Colin Taylor-Evans, was in town. He spends half the year in Laos helping kids at the blind school in Vientiane. He speaks Lao and was a great help. He has total recall and knows few boundaries.

Colin liked to play soccer with the kids and they loved his style. The ball needed to be encased in a plastic bag so he could hear it coming. He is blind, after all. That little setback hasn't stopped him from doing anything except, perhaps, driving. In Luang Prabang he is known as Colin #1.

Lao School Holidays

The following week saw the start of school holidays in Laos. Of the 600 plus students at the orphanage school, about 240 didn't have anywhere to call home. These kids had no family and no welcoming village, so they stayed at the school with very limited supervision and facilities. One sticky rice meal a day was prepared in the steaming room and the children received a small allowance to buy some thin vegetable soup to have with the rice.

A number of volunteers support the food improvement program with donations of eggs, fish, meat and vegetables. This may provide a hot meal one or two days a week for the holiday period; but was all very ad hoc.

We became aware of a food and health improvement program run by an Australian expat, who owned a very smart boutique villa in town. This program was newly commenced that first year we visited Luang Prabang but we were unable to connect with the guy who was setting this up. Clearly, to commence any officially sanctioned assistance program for the orphanage school, all sorts of government approvals are essential. Very challenging, indeed.

Meanwhile, Tou and Phay were so moved they offered to organise a major 'cook up' for the kids and we bought the produce. They borrowed huge pots from one of the temples and hired two cooks, while we supplied the fish and vegetables. The steaming room was again in full swing when our little golf carts pulled up at the orphanage. We had to serve off the back of the carts as the pots were too big to move.

Again, the gong sounded and the kids lined up with their bowls and their big smiles.

A much welcomed lunch was served.

During the holiday break Seng Song was running extra art classes to help those kids who showed interest.

He encouraged us to stay and watch the classes in action. He had two standout students, Kong Lee and Croisant, plus several budding young artists.

Our villa welcomed some new Aussie guests and at dinner we met Libby and Glen Morrison, who were regular visitors to this part of the world, along with their fellow traveller, Jeanette Tyler. We roped them into helping out at the next orphanage 'nosh up', along with Colin.

As It turned out, Libby and Glen lived very close to us in Melbourne, and we regularly get together.

Jeanette lived in NSW and as a teacher, loved interacting with the children.

We all agreed to meet in Luang Prabang, same time, next year.

Our first month in Laos was no holiday. It was an experience that will stay with us forever.

Laos

Laos

27 - IT'S DEFINITELY LAOS

According to Australia Post, Laos does not exist.

A young student I met asked me where I lived. 'Melbourne, Australia' I replied. That's pretty difficult to comprehend by someone who has never travelled further than the next village in rural Laos. I decided to send him a basic student atlas as I couldn't purchase one in Luang Prabang. Back home I packed an envelope with an easy-to-read atlas and headed down to my local post office. I had labelled it with the student's name and contact details, care of the Luang Prabang Post Office, LAOS.

Most Lao people do not have a private mail address, let alone a bank account.

When I went to mail it off my post office said Laos wasn't in the system. They suggested Vietnam, Cambodia or Myanmar. Yes, they are bordering independent countries, but not what we need. "No, It's definitely Laos", I insisted.

A few phone calls later and we settled on 'The Peoples Democratic Republic of Laos'. (That's strange; because there's nothing democratic about Laos.)

I caught up with this young guy on our next visit and he said he just loved his book of maps. It's sad, but most likely that the only overseas travel he will ever experience will be in his mind.

We had many people we wanted to reconnect with back in LP including our Aussie crew from last year.

Word had gone out that I was a video maker (of sorts) and I was asked if I could document the work of a fair trade silk project, titled 'Mulberries' (check it out on YouTube).

This project involved a number of us Aussies joining a Lao team to head off in two minivans to remote villages in the north. It was a week of amazing experiences, not so comfortable accommodation and very challenging eating options.

On this and subsequent trips we learned much about the country's dark history, particularly relating to the Vietnam war. America (CIA) dropped more bombs per square mile here than on any other country on earth.

Massive bombing raids were conducted between 1964 and 1973. Much unexploded ordnance remains and takes innocent lives to this day. The locals were reticent to speak out even through a trusted interpreter. That speaks volumes. This is a communist country with strong military enforcers.

On our fourth annual expedition we finally met up with Andrew Brown. He's the guy who ran the boutique villa in town and was involved in food and health improvement programs at three orphanage schools and a number of remote villages.

Each year he seemed to be spending less time on the villa and more on his chosen projects. I offered to make video programs to support his fundraising efforts abroad. Lynn and I also became involved in supporting the projects in the out-of-town orphanages. Andrew married a Lao woman, sold his interest in the villa and expanded his humanitarian projects. He set up a college sponsorship program for students graduating from the orphanage schools (please visit www.supportlaochildren.com).

How Now...Speak Lao

I came up with a plan to publish a little Lao word guide for foreigners. I prepared a list of everyday English words that would be valuable to have the Lao translation. I formed a panel of English-speaking and bilingual friends. Along with Colin, who is conversational in Lao, we had a couple of novice monks and a teacher from LEOT (Lao Educational Opportunities Trust) English language school. The plan was to spell out each word or phrase in English, Lao and phonetically. The A6 booklet is printed locally and made available for sale by Lao people to support Lao people. They pay 50 cents per copy and sell for $1 with the first 4 copies free to the seller. The project is in its fourth year and is self funding.

In town, Lynn also loves the twice-daily English conversation sessions at Big Brother Mouse (BBM) library.

Everyone's welcome to talk and read with young Lao students, many of whom were novice monks. BBM introduced the first books to be published in the Lao language. Their story is on my YouTube channel.

(I hope they don't take this stuff down when I leave the building.)

Our ongoing interests in Laos are with Andrew Brown's projects under the banner 'Support Lao Children', and the amazing work under the leadership of Peter Banwell at LEOT. This latter identity is worth an entire chapter, but I'll spare you all the detail, except to say that Jeanette Tyler, whom we met in LP on our first visit, now runs the LEOT school and she's one year older than me...shy of one day. She's a real dynamo.

Sorry to go on, but this also needs mentioning...LEOT was set up by a group of British business people headed by Peter Banwell, a true gentleman if ever I've met one. After a hot day's work, Peter likes to relax with a G & T. That's a sure sign of a true gentleman.

Another equally valuable sign of a gentleman is one who owns a set of bagpipes, but doesn't play them.

I have posted a number video programs I made over many years of visiting Luang Prabang on my YouTube channel.

The best way to cross the Mekong in Luang Prabang is on the car/motorbike ferry. The wet season (mid year) offers added excitement.

Our little Lao world guide

Above: Seng Song

Above left Colin #1 and Lynn (left) wuth their Big Brother Mouse students

28 - HAWAII

In 2012 Lynn and I travelled with Libby and Glen to Hawaii. They are highly experienced globetrotters and Libby always plans their overseas trips to the nth degree. We toured four islands in five weeks. This excursion did get off to a wobbly start when our Qantas flight had to be diverted to Nadi, Fiji, due to a cracked windscreen. Fiji put on the worst possible weather and our twenty-four-hour layover was very nearly a week, but for a short break in the weather that allowed our flight to continue on. The landscaped, lavishly appointed resorts of Honolulu attract tourists from all over the world. American seniors prefer the cruise ships with the organised side trips and the all-you-can-eat banquets, and that's just for lunch! We couldn't wait to get out into the real Hawaiian countryside...and it was beautiful. The highlight of the tour, or maybe I could describe it as a bootcamp, was our time around the active volcano Kilauea, on the Island of Kauai. With our guide, 'Lava Cheryl', we hiked out across two kilometres of volcanic lava in the Kalapana region until we came to an active flow. It was slow moving and extremely dangerous, but our guide knew the territory and we felt quite safe. Kilauea had been active from 1983 to 2018. We were there in 2012 and the warnings were increasing. In 2018 its activity peaked and lava flows destroyed 700 homes and added 350 acres of new land to the Island of Hawaii. The spectacular scenery on each of the four Islands we visited has provided the setting for many, many major motion pictures. The tourist guide maps show the shooting locations of some of the amazing productions, including Jurassic Park, South Pacific and Raiders of the Lost Ark. Had we been there in earlier days I may well have been a Hollywood extra.

The Big Island in the State of Hawaii offers an interesting insight to the vulnerability of volcanic activity resulting in tsunamis. The town of Hilo is only a few metres above sea level and all along the lower coastlines are enormous towers with horn speakers ready to sound the tsunami warning. The town has a tatty little museum that tells the story of the devastating 1960 tsunami.

For me, the big attraction of this region is the Hilo Horseshoe Pitching Club. Also known as 'Throwing Iron'.

The pitch has a vertical metal rod at each end and the player has to toss the horseshoe and hit the rod, then turn around and have a crack at the other end. It's not a great spectator sport. When the locals aren't chucking horseshoes around, many are out in the shed fitting oversize wheels on their super-high suspension pick-ups. American flags were everywhere including on flagpoles in private front gardens.

A memorable, large roadside billboard declared 'Don't Think...PRAY'.

Only in America? Please don't tell me that they behave like this in Queensland.

Considering that we first met Libby and Glen in Laos and toured that country with them, this excursion was a mind blowing contrast for each of us.

29 - MYANMAR

Prior to attending to our now regular Luang Prabang activities we planned a side trip to Myanmar. When I say 'we planned', read Libby did most of the planning. Myanmar (formerly Burma) was slowly opening up to tourists although travellers were cautioned to plan ahead and avoid certain regions. We were warned not to book 'all-inclusive' holiday packages and ensure our tourism dollars didn't end up in the pockets of military junta and their cronies. Eating at street vendor stalls was best avoided unless you planned to engage in a violent weight loss program!

Our Air Asia flight landed us in Yangon on 31st December 2012. As advised, we carried freshly minted US dollars in a wide range of denominations. In many circumstances we needed to tender the exact amount.

We were all pretty familiar with travelling in the Third World, but Myanmar nudged the experience up a notch. The public transport system was totally run down and safety was not a demonstrated priority. In some cities and larger townships, motor cycles are banned. The reason is said to be that they can breed motorcycle gangs and be used in robberies. I hadn't planned to hire a motorbike, or commit a robbery for that matter.

Glenn and Libby in Myanmar

The little children at this prep class sang 'Head and shoulders, knees and toes' in their best English.

30 - WHO'S SCOOTER?

Just winding back the clock for a moment; when Kylie-Ann was a toddler I used to turn my hands into finger puppets and make up silly little stories. The middle finger (tall man) was the neck and head while the other four digits were the legs. Ky would roar with laughter. She named the little fellow 'Shoolfer'. When Katie and Em arrived on the scene, they joined in. I played Shoolfer puppets with all their little mates and with my friends' and relatives' little ones.

Even Liv and Mattis in Switzerland loved the exaggerated animated nonsense. Years later, my grandchildren, Lenny and Courtney, motivated me to bring Shoolfer out of retirement.

In 2017 I decided to bring the characters to life in book format. I can't draw for nuts! I wrote the first story, 'Shoolfer loves finger painting'. Lynn arranged for her two great-nieces, Millie and Zoe, to come over and do some finger painting so that I could try the story line out. The session went well. The girls had fun and I had some great pics of their little hand puppets. I wrote three little story lines and now I needed a graphic artist to move the project on.

I used an on-line platform to connect to the right person. I viewed quite a few on-line portfolios and narrowed it down to four potential artists. The standout artist was a young Japanese woman, Satoko Higashi, who was studying English in Queensland. She had also taught little kids 'hip-hop' dancing in my once home town of Echuca. What are the chances...?

Together, via email and dropbox, we worked on the three titles over two years and I had 20 copies of each printed for evaluation by a group of toddlers and kindergarten/ lower primary school children. The glaring problem was the main character's name was not easy remember. I consulted my main mentor, Richard.

He came up with 'Scooter'. Perfect Rick.

So, now as I write, I continue to work on fine-tuning, re-testing and finding a publisher. This series will be bigger than Peppa Pig and Thomas The Tank Engine, so all potential publishers, please form a double queue at our front door. Please!

Scooter with our little Corkie

31 - CHAMPASAK, LAOS

In 2018 we decided to have Christmas in Luang Prabang as we had the previous year.

Our group comprised a number of volunteers from countries including Australia, New Zealand, Canada, United States and of course, The Peoples Democratic Republic of Laos.

Again, our friends from Mt Zero in the western district of Victoria met us there. Jane and Neil Seymour had accompanied us on a side trip in 2017.

I had the urge to film the elusive, and almost extinct, Irrawaddy fresh river dolphins down in the Four Thousand Islands archipelago, where Cambodia meets Laos on the mighty Mekong.

After a couple of weeks doing our thing in LP, the four of us took the Air Lao flight south, to Pakse.

Pakse! so good they named it once.

After a few days exploring the ancient temple ruins and other attractions we headed further south in a crowded minivan to the Champasak region. Our destination was the Island of Don Khon, a thirty-minute ride in a flat-bottom, uncomfortable, leaky, wooden boat. The tiny amount of freeboard meant we were sitting just above the waterline. The island's main attraction is the Li Phi Falls (also called Tat Samphamit Waterfalls). By now we've turned the clock back another 25 years from Luang Prabang. The scenery is truly spectacular with very few farlung (foreigners) in sight. There are no cars on the island. The way to get around is by walking, bike riding or on a rusty, old, worn-out tuk-tuk. The roads are pot-holed bush tracks and after a rain shower, are very difficult to negotiate.

Our last few days were made even more challenging owing to a rogue water buffalo tripping over the main water supply hose. This meant no water in the bathroom or toilets for a day or so. No one appeared too stressed. No point. Lao people take everything in their stride: even more so in this remote region.

The day before we were to leave the Island, Jane decided she just had to hire a bike and venture out. Just after sunset, a pot hole jumped out and grabbed her front wheel and over she went. Jane was battered, bruised and not travelling well.

The unmanned first aid post wasn't much use and Neil had to use all his 'Google Translate' skills to muster emergency treatment. The next day Jane had to be assisted on to an armchair and carried onto the flat bottom boat for the trip back across the river to our minivan. She did rise to the occasion and gave what could only be described as a 'Royal wave' to the bewildered onlookers. The minivan was driven down to the Mekong river bank and the chair, complete with a smiling Jane, was taken off the boat. We all had a fairly uncomfortable trip back to Pakse, but nowhere as uncomfortable as Jane's, and then by air to Luang Prabang. Travel insurance cut in and they returned to Australia bruised but not beaten.

32 - UPDATE DIGITAL

This was a little retirement business I set up after retiring from Newmarket Music a decade ago. It was primarily an analogue to digital service with the main target market to be transferring VHS tapes to DVD format.

Babies in the bath, tedious, poorly filmed boring wedding ceremonies and dreadfully embarrassing travel tapes paid the rent. I won't go on about the appalling school dance and drama concerts because as a parent of three budding young dancers, I've been there-done that. When it's your own kids, it's different (yet still painful to have to sit through).

Update Digital proved to be a nice little earner and as the years went on, this micro, part-time business extended its service repertoire. I took in a partner as I didn't want to work full time and the workload was increasing and thankfully, becoming more diverse.

We moved the business into a shop in McKinnon and offered transfers of any format to DVD, CD and/or USB drives.

I was also providing video editing and production services. Davido and I each worked two or three days a week, more if required. The plan was to keep the business as a little retirement, pocket-money top up unit.

I set the shop up like a TV studio with a lighting grid and retro equipment on display. It was my ideal man cave but for the deteriorating state of the building. As time went on the landlord reluctantly carried out some maintenance to a very poor standard. The building leaked after a decent rainfall and the plumbing was Third World standard. I referred to the outside toilet as the executive bathroom. The tap water wasn't drinkable even if boiled. Davido tried to work with this horrid fellow to get things improved, but he somehow always managed to get stuck in nasty fellow's craw.

In late December 2019 Lynn and I set off for another tour of duty in Laos. Again we organised to have Christmas lunch in Luang Prabang with the usual suspects. Our Canadian friend, Stephen Ariss, couldn't make it this time and was much missed as my late-night vino buddy.

Andrew Brown (Support Lao Children) had just opened a creche at the school for orphaned infants and toddlers, and Lynn with her kindergarten teaching experience was authorised to get involved. I made a video for the fundraising website. The plan was to leave Laos in late January, and have a stopover in Perth on the way home.

We always needed a debriefing period after spending time in LP.

On New Year's Eve we planned a sunset cruise on the Mekong, followed by dinner on the banks.

I checked my email late in the day, just before heading down to the Mekong, and there was a message from Davido.

He'd had an ongoing SMS run in with the landlord and we were given one months notice to vacate the shop. I had a commitment to a number of projects in Laos that took me up until late January and then we planned to return via Singapore and Perth. We hadn't booked a return flight from Perth to Melbourne. We were thinking about February 12-15th 2020. Otherwise all flights were locked in and very expensive to change.

I asked Davido to explain to the landlord that I was overseas as a volunteer and we would appreciate an extension for two months and an opportunity to discuss alternatives. We'd been leasing this shop for about seven years and never missed paying the rent on time, but this fellow further bombarded Davido with a tirade of insults. I always avoided the man as I thought Davido had his measure. Clearly not, and this guy almost destroyed my offsider with his toxic communications. We had to move as we knew the landlord would not hesitate to lock us out on February first. He was indeed, a nasty piece of work!

Emails went to and fro and it was apparent that my workmate was at breaking point. His emails were distressing and literally a cry for help. I arranged for a 'Man with a Van' to pack up and remove all our equipment, but Davido was required to find some temporary space.

I contacted our friends Rod and Jenny as they had offered any assistance with any matter when we left Melbourne.

In the meantime, every short-term rental Davido tried to tee up fell over and he rented two expensive storage units nearby. Rod co-ordinated the shift, and the business was put on ice! Davido informed me that he did take home some equipment so he could continue to offer a much restricted service; after all, his phone number was plastered all over the shopfront.

We returned to Perth as scheduled on January 28th 2020, abandoned our holiday plans and flew back home on January 30th. I had one day to pack up the last of my treasures and get them into storage. Rod, Jenny, Davido and I had a debriefing coffee and my workmate presented me the bill for the first months storage fee of $720.

    I was very grateful to the team for bringing the project to a conclusion; for now, at least. I thinned out the stored furniture and equipment and condensed it to one unit after many trips to opportunity shops and erecycling facilities. A friend offered me free storage space and, as I write, my gear is stashed away until I formulate a new business plan...if ever.

33 - MONDAY ONE DAY, MONDAY THE NEXT

2020 and COVID-19 comes along to turn the world upside down. We would have had to close down our little not-for-profit* business had we battled on. Every cloud...and all that!

* The not-for-profit component was not part of the original business plan.

Now we're moving in and out of months of lockdown in Melbourne, yet we still have to mask up when leaving the house. Victorians are prohibited from visiting most other Australian states without a fourteen day quarantine period and same applies in the opposite direction.

Lynn and I are so fortunate to have a lovely home and a productive garden that offers joyful distraction.

We have wonderful friends and neighbours. My cooking skills have progressed to four signature dishes, three of which, so I'm advised, aren't too bad.

I have mastered the art of completing one hours workload in just six hours.

There's a certain truth to the concept of a COVID fog. As lockdowns open and close worldwide, the future is seems uncertain for so many. Australia is very well placed, going forward.

Oh, how I detest that going forward weasel phrase.

Similarly, for what it's worth, at the end of the day, all things being equal, I shall avoid cliches like the plague.

However, I am looking forward to writing more chapters.

Lynn's very wise aunt Ellen always said..."play nicely."

*

John Bye • 0422 139 444
johnbyeproductions@gmail.com

www.ingramcontent.com/pod-product-compliance
Lightning Source LLC
Chambersburg PA
CBHW050315010526
44107CB00055B/2250